365 Fun Facts Book
for Kids and Adults

365 Fun Facts Book for Kids and Adults

A Fun and Engaging Book of Interesting Facts About Science, History, Space, and More. Perfect for Kids Ages 8-12 and Adults Who Love Learning Every Day!

Grace Henderson

The content contained within this book may not be reproduced, duplicated or transmitted without direct written permission from the author or the publisher.

Under no circumstances will any blame or legal responsibility be held against the publisher, or author, for any damages, reparation, or monetary loss due to the information contained within this book. Either directly or indirectly. You are responsible for your own choices, actions, and results.

Legal Notice:

This book is copyright protected. This book is only for personal use. You cannot amend, distribute, sell, use, quote or paraphrase any part, or the content within this book, without the consent of the author or publisher.

Disclaimer Notice:

Please note the information contained within this document is for educational and entertainment purposes only. All effort has been executed to present accurate, up to date, and reliable, complete information. No warranties of any kind are declared or implied. Readers acknowledge that the author is not engaging in the rendering of legal, financial, medical or professional advice. The content within this book has been derived from various sources. Please consult a licensed professional before attempting any techniques outlined in this book.

By reading this document, the reader agrees that under no circumstances is the author responsible for any losses, direct or indirect, which are incurred as a result of the use of the information contained within this document, including, but not limited to, — errors, omissions, or inaccuracies.

Table of Contents

1. Great inventions
1.1. What We Use in Everyday Life

1. Modern matches were invented in 1827 by a British scientist named John Walker, who came up with a cool idea. He made little wooden sticks with special tips that would catch fire if you rubbed them against something rough, like sandpaper. These were the first matches. People called them "friction lights."

2. Later on, in the 1830s, a French chemist, **Charles Sauria,** created matches using a **special chemical** called **white phosphorus.** These matches were easier to ignite, but the white phosphorus was really bad for people's health. Luckily, a Swedish guy named **Johan Lundstrom** made matches much safer in 1855. He used a different kind of phosphorus that was not that harmful.

3. Austria was one of the first countries to use postcards. In 1869, they introduced these special cards that you could use to send short messages. People loved how convenient and affordable they were. Before long, postcards were all the rage across Europe. It is impressive how something so simple has been around for so long!

4. A long time ago, **puzzles** were created to help kids learn, not just for fun. In the 1700s, a guy named John Spilsbury made **the first puzzle.** He cut up a map of Europe to help kids learn geography. It was a clever idea! Over time, puzzles became more fun and less about learning, but they are still a great way to pass the time.

7

5. A long time ago, in 1736–1746, a French explorer named **Charles Marie de la Condamine** traveled to South America. During his travels, he saw Native Americans collecting a sticky substance from trees. This substance was called **rubber.** When he went back to Europe, he brought some rubber with him. People started experimenting with it. They found that if they added sulfur and heated it up, they could make rubber much stronger.

6. Before printing presses, books had to be written by hand. But around 1440, Johannes Gutenberg invented **the first printing press.** His invention used movable pieces of metal with letters on them, which made printing books much faster and cheaper. **Gutenberg's printing press** helped start a time called the Renaissance when people were curious about the world and wanted to learn as much as they could.

7. Imagine a world without tall buildings or solid bridges. It might seem strange, but a long time ago, people did not have the materials we use today to build these things. A French man named **Joseph Monier** changed all that **in 1849.** He invented **reinforced concrete,** the material that became the basis of the modern construction industry. Joseph wanted to make plant pots more durable, so he added iron bars to the concrete. **In 1867,** Monier patented his idea and expanded its use to beams, pipes, and building structures. Today, reinforced concrete helps build sturdy buildings and bridges.

1.2. Electricity

8. An ancient experiment with electricity: a Greek scientist named Thales noticed something strange around 600 BC. When he rubbed amber, a yellow stone, with a piece of wool, it started to stick to tiny things. It was one of the earliest discoveries about static electricity.

9. In 1752, a brilliant scientist named Benjamin Franklin conducted a famous kite experiment. He wanted to find out if lightning was electricity. He flew a kite during a thunderstorm. When lightning struck the kite, it traveled down a string and into a key that Franklin was holding. It was a pretty risky experiment, but it proved that lightning is a form of electricity.

10. Did you know that batteries were not always around? In 1800, a scientist named Alessandro Volta created **the first battery.** He called it a voltaic pile. This invention was a huge step forward for science because it enabled us to make electricity.

11. In 1831, a scientist named Michael Faraday discovered something interesting about electricity and magnets. He found out that you could make electricity with a magnet if you moved it around a wire. This discovery, called **electromagnetic induction,** is the principle behind the work of generators and transformers.

12. Did you know that **Thomas Edison** invented **the light bulb?** In 1879, he made a light bulb with a thin piece of carbon inside. This made the bulb that could stay lit for a long time. Edison made lots of these light bulbs and sold them to people so they could have light in their homes whenever they wanted.

13. **In 1887,** a brilliant scientist named **Nikola Tesla** helped develop **alternating current** (AC) electricity. It could power bigger things and travel farther. This invention changed the world and is why we have electricity in our homes today.

1.3. Radio, Telephone, Cinema, and Other Devices

14. The telephone was invented almost 150 years ago! In 1876, **Alexander Graham Bell** created a machine that sent voices over wires. This invention was a big deal because it allowed people to talk to each other even if they were far away.

15. However, another person might have invented the telephone before Bell. An Italian man named **Antonio Meucci** made a **similar device in the 1850s**. But he did not get a patent for it. So, even though Meucci might have had the idea first, Bell is the one who is officially known as the inventor of the telephone because he was the first to get a patent and make it widely used.

16. The first mobile phone was invented **by Martin Cooper in 1973.** It was called the Motorola DynaTAC, and it was huge and weighed 5.5 pounds, so one needed two hands to hold it, and the battery only lasted 20 minutes.

17. In 1983, Motorola made **the DynaTAC 8000X, the first cell phone people could buy.** It was large, about the size of a brick, and cost a lot of money - around **$4,000**! Anyway, it was the beginning of everyone having a cell phone.

18. Smartphones like the ones we use today became popular **in the 1990s.** The first one was called the **IBM Simon.** It came out **in 1994** and had a touchscreen. It could do things like send emails and texts and even keep track of your schedule, just like our phones today. It was the beginning of a significant change in how we use technology.

19. Did you know that taking pictures was not always as easy as it is today? In 1839, **Louis Daguerre** invented a revolutionary way to take pictures. His invention, the **daguerreotype**, used special metal plates that were coated with silver to capture images. That was the start of **photography** as we know it today.

20. In 1895, two brothers, **Louis and Auguste Lumière,** invented a special machine called a cinematograph that could take pictures and show them on a big screen. Their **first movie,** "Arrival of a Train at La Ciotat," was shown on December 28, 1895, in Paris, France. This was the beginning of the movie industry!

21. The invention of the radio was a big deal, and **a few smart people worked on it. In 1895,** an Italian named **Guglielmo Marconi** sent the first radio signal over a long distance and got a patent for his invention. Around the same time, a Russian scientist named **Alexander Popov** made a radio receiver.

Meanwhile, a famous inventor **Nikola Tesla** was experimenting with wireless signals. Together, these scientists helped us have radios today.

22. Did you know that you can thank **Thomas Edison** for being able to listen to your favorite songs on your phone? **In 1877**, he invented the **phonograph**, the first machine that could record sound. It was a big deal at the time because people could hear their voices and listen to music whenever they wanted!

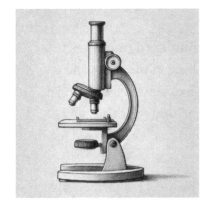

23. The first microscope was made by two Dutch guys named **Zacharias** and **Hans Janssen** in the late 1500s. Their microscope used two lenses to make things look bigger. Later, a scientist named **Antonie van Leeuwenhoek** made microscopes so powerful that he could see tiny living things that no one had ever seen before. He was the first person to see tiny living things, like bacteria.

24. Have you ever heard of **Galileo Galilei**? He was a very intelligent man who loved to look at the stars. In 1609, he made a tool that was like a telescope, but he used it to look at tiny things. He called it an "**occhiolino**," which means "little eye." Even though it was not a perfect microscope, Galileo's invention was crucial for helping us understand how to make things look bigger.

1.4. Computers and the Internet

25. Computers were not always small. **In the 1830s, Charles Babbage** designed a giant machine called **the Analytical Engine**. This machine could perform arithmetic calculations and store information. So, it was like the great-great-grandfather of the computers we use today.

26. Did you know that one of **the first computer programmers** was a woman? Her name was **Ada Lovelace**. She lived in the 1800s and worked with **Charles Babbage** on his machine, the Analytical Engine. In 1843, Ada wrote notes that described an **algorithm** for calculating Bernoulli numbers on this machine. This algorithm is considered the first computer program ever written.

27. **Alan Turing** was a mathematician and a scientist who figured out how computers could work. **In 1936**, he formulated an idea for a special type of machine called a **Turing machine**, which became the basis for the theory of algorithms and computers. During World War II, Turing helped **break a secret code** that the Germans were using. His work helped to end the war. His work was the foundation for modern computing and artificial intelligence theory.

28. **The first electronic computers** were invented in **the 1940s**. One of the first computers was called **ENIAC**. It was built in 1945 in the United States. It was so big that it filled up a whole room! ENIAC could do about **5,000 calculations every second**.

29. **In 1947**, some intelligent scientists named **John Bardeen, Walter Brattain**, and **William Shockley** invented a transistor. This tiny part made it possible to create much smaller and more powerful electronic devices.

30. **Hedy Lamarr** was not just a famous movie star—she was also a brilliant inventor. During World War II, **In 1941**, with **George Antheil**, a composer, she developed a system of **frequency dispersion**, a way to send secret radio messages that were secure from intercepting. Her invention is the foundation for many wireless technologies we use today, like **Wi-Fi, Bluetooth,** and **GPS**.

31. In 1971, **Intel** made **the first microchip** that could power an entire computer. It was called the **Intel 4004**. This chip was significant because it made computers much smaller and cheaper to make. Thanks to the Intel 4004, we can have powerful computers in our homes and schools.

32. **In the 1970s**, people started making computers **small enough** for anyone **to use at home**. One of the very first home computers was called **the Altair 8800**. It was released **in 1973** and changed the way we use computers.

33. Did you know that Apple computers started in a garage? **In 1976, Steve Jobs** and **Steve Wozniak** built the first Apple computer right in their garage. It was called the **Apple I**, one of the first personal computers. This was the beginning of the company that changed the world.

34. **In 1981, IBM** made a new type of computer that people could use at home. It was called **the IBM PC**.

This computer was so popular that it became the standard for all other computers. It used a software called MS-DOS from Microsoft, which made it easy for people to use. Thanks to the IBM PC, computers became a big part of our lives.

35. Can you imagine a world without the Internet? Well, it all started in **1969** with something called **ARPANET**. It was a network that connected computers at different places, like universities and government buildings. ARPANET used a **specific method** of sending information and letting computers "talk" to each other across long distances. This network was like the grandfather of the Internet we use today.

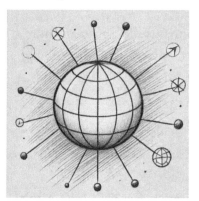

36. In 1989, a scientist named **Tim Berners-Lee** created the **World Wide Web.** He made it possible to connect different pages on the internet together using links so we could easily find information. This is how we got the World Wide Web!

37. The Internet started to be used for **businesses and shopping** in **the 1990s**. A company called **America Online (AOL)** started a service that let people connect to the internet from their homes, and **Amazon** began selling things online. So people could buy almost anything online. This was the beginning of online shopping, which made the internet a big part of our lives.

1.5. Medicine

38. Before the 1840s, surgery was scary and painful. But then, doctors discovered **anesthesia**. Anesthesia is a special kind of medicine that makes you go to sleep during surgery so you do not feel any pain. It is like magic, and it has saved countless lives.

39. **X-rays** are like super-powerful flashlights that can see through your body. A scientist named Wilhelm Röntgen invented them in 1895. X-rays help doctors see what occurs inside your body without surgery. They are used to check for broken bones, find cavities in your teeth, and diagnose various medical problems.

40. Vitamin C is a tiny but mighty vitamin! Scientists **Frederick Hopkins and Thomas F. G. Higham discovered** it back in **1932**. It is like a secret ingredient that helps our bodies work efficiently. Vitamin C helps our immune system stay strong. This helps us fight off colds and other illnesses. It also helps our bodies heal when we get hurt.

41. People did not always know how blood moved around their bodies. A long time ago, in 1628, a doctor named **William Harvey** figured it out. He discovered that **blood travels in a circle**, going to the heart and then back out to the rest of the body. This finding was a crucial discovery that helped us understand how our bodies work.

42. **Robert Koch** was a bright German doctor who studied tiny germs. He figured out that **different germs cause different diseases**, and he developed rules to help other scientists find out which germs cause which diseases. His work was so important that he won a Nobel Prize in 1905.

43. A long time ago, there were no **antiseptics,** and doctors used to make people sick after surgery as they did not know how to keep things clean. But **in 1865**, a doctor named **Joseph Lister** figured out how to kill germs. He used carbolic acid to clean his tools and wounds. His method helped to save a lot of lives.

44. In 1885, a scientist named **Louis Pasteur** created a special medicine to protect people from a terrifying disease called **rabies**. A young boy named **Joseph Meister** was the first person to get this medicine, and it saved his life.

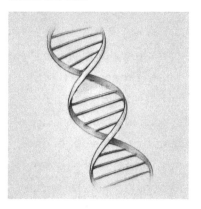

45. Everything about you, from your eye color to your height, is stored in tiny things inside your cells. These things are called **DNA**. DNA was discovered by a scientist named **Friedrich Miescher in 1869**. His discovery helped us understand how we inherit traits from our parents.

46. In 1966, two scientists named Har Gobind Khorana and Marshall Nirenberg cracked **the genetic code**, which is like a set of instructions written in our DNA on how to make proteins.

47. Diabetes used to be a very serious disease, but **in 1921**, two scientists, **Frederick Banting** and **Charles Best**, discovered **insulin**. Insulin is a special medicine that helps the body use sugar. Thanks to their discovery, millions of people are alive today.

1.6. Food Storage and Sanitation

48. Refrigerators have changed our lives in a big way! Before refrigerators, food would go bad really quickly. They were invented in the **1830s** and have become a part of our kitchens. Now, we can keep our food cold and fresh for much longer. **Refrigeration** helps us avoid getting sick from spoiled food and lets us eat a wider variety of foods.

49. Canned food was not always around, but in 1804, a French chef named **Nicolas Appert** invented a way to keep food fresh for a long time. He put food in glass jars and heated them to kill the germs. Later, **in 1810**, a man named **Peter Durand** made it even better by using metal cans.

50. Have you ever wondered how milk stays fresh for so long? A long time ago, a scientist named **Louis Pasteur** discovered an effective way to keep liquids safe. This process is called pasteurization. It involves heating liquids to a specific temperature to destroy harmful microorganisms without changing the taste or nutritional properties of the product. Pasteur developed the method to prevent wine and beer from spoiling, but **pasteurization** later became widely used to treat milk and other types of drinks and foods, making it safe for consumption and extending their shelf life.

51. Can you imagine living in a city without clean water or a way to get rid of dirty water? Before **sewers and water systems,** cities had no clean water or proper waste disposal, which made people sick. These systems helped make cities cleaner and safer.

52. The Romans were advanced engineers! Around 600 BC, they built one of the first sewer systems to keep cities clean. It was a network of **underground tunnels that carried away dirty water and rainwater.** This not only helped keep Rome clean but also helped it grow and become a powerful city. Many of the sewer systems we have today are based on their design.

1.7. Various Transport

53. The wheel is one of the greatest inventions ever! People started using wheels in **Mesopotamia** a long time ago, around **3500 BC**. They used them for making pots and then for building carts and wagons. The wheel was a simple but brilliant invention that changed the world.

54. People in **Ancient Egypt** were using **boats** and **ships** as early as **3000 BC**. They used long, wooden boats to travel up and down the Nile River. These boats were used for everything from trade to travel.

55. Did you know that **ancient Egyptians** used **chariots** to go to war? They started using chariots around **1600 BC**. These were like fast, moving platforms pulled by horses for archers and spear throwers. The chariot was a symbol of strength and bravery in ancient Egypt.

56. In 1879, a smart guy named **Gottlieb Daimler** invented the first electric tram. It was like a mini electric train that traveled along the streets. It was a big step forward for transportation.

57. The first mechanically propelled submarine was invented by **Robert Fulton in 1800**. He called it the **Nautilus**. It was like a secret underwater ship that could be used for war and showed that people could travel underwater.

58. The helicopter was invented **in 1939 by Igor Sikorsky**, a Ukrainian-American. His helicopter, the **VS-300,** was the first successful helicopter that could take off and land straight up and down. It made flying way cooler and created new possibilities for air travel.

59. In 1783, **the Montgolfier brothers** in France made a significant discovery: **hot air rises**! They used this principle to build a large balloon. By heating the air inside, they could make it lighter than the air outside, causing the balloon to lift off. Their first successful flight lasted approximately 25 minutes, reaching an altitude of around 3,000 feet and traveling about 5.5 miles. This exciting event marked the start of air travel as we know it!

60. Before **1807**, traveling by water was slow and often challenging. But that all changed when American inventor **Robert Fulton** introduced **the first successful steamboat**. His boat made its first trip up the Hudson River, traveling about 150 miles from New York City to Albany in 32 hours. It used a steam engine to power two giant paddle wheels, each 15 feet across! This exciting event changed everything about water travel, making it much faster and more efficient, as it launched the era of steamboats.

61. **The bicycle** was invented **in the early 1800s**. The first version was kind of like a scooter, called a **"dandy horse"** or **"draisine"** made in 1817 by a German baron named Karl von Drais. It was a two-wheeled vehicle that riders moved by pushing off the ground with their feet. A significant advancement came in the 1860s when French inventors **Pierre and Ernest Michaux** introduced pedals to the front wheel. But it was not until the **1880s** that the bicycle we know today took shape.

A British inventor, **John Kemp Starley**, invented the "safety bicycle" with a chain that powered the back wheel. This invention made it much safer and easier to ride, and that is why most bicycles today use the same design.

62. The first car was invented **in 1886** by a German engineer named **Karl Benz**. He built a three-wheeled vehicle with a gasoline-powered engine called the **Benz Patent-Motorwagen**. This amazing invention was the first car that could move itself!

63. While Karl Benz was busy building his three-wheeled car, two other brilliant minds in Germany, **Gottlieb Daimler** and **Wilhelm Maybach**, were also working on a big idea: a four-wheeled vehicle powered by a similar gasoline engine. These inventions by Benz, Daimler, and Maybach sparked the birth of the automobile industry, which changed transportation and factories around the world.

64. Henry Ford did not invent the car, but he changed how they were made. **In 1913**, he came up with a brilliant idea: **the moving assembly line**. It made building cars much faster and less expensive, so more families could finally buy their cars. The **Ford Model T**, which his company had launched in 1908, became incredibly popular because it was affordable for many Americans.

1.8. Scientists and Their Contribution to Science

65. For a long time, people believed the Earth was the center of the universe and everything else, including the Sun, moved around it. **Nicolaus Copernicus** was the first to come up with the idea that **the Earth goes around the Sun.** He shared this idea in 1543. Later, scientists like Galileo Galilei, Johannes Kepler, and others used telescopes and math to prove Copernicus's idea was correct, changing our understanding of the universe forever.

66. The Nobel Prize is a famous award, but there is a mystery about it. What is the reason for no Nobel prize in mathematics? One idea is that **Alfred Nobel**, the guy who started the prize, wanted to reward things that had real-world use. Maybe because there are other prizes for math, like the Fields Medal, or he probably did not like math!

67. In 1666, Isaac Newton made a groundbreaking discovery that would forever change our understanding of the universe: **the law of universal gravitation.** There is a popular story about an apple falling from a tree that supposedly got him thinking about this force.

However, Newton's work took years of careful study and complex math. He realized that this is the force that keeps the Moon orbiting Earth and the Earth orbiting the Sun. He published his findings **in 1687.** This discovery was a breakthrough and explained how things move in the universe.

68. An English scientist named **Charles Darwin** developed the theory of evolution and published it **in 1859**. Darwin suggested that all living things shared a common ancestor and had changed over millions of years through a process he called natural selection. It means that if an animal has a trait that helps it survive, it is more likely to live long enough to have babies who also have the trait. Amazingly, another scientist, **Alfred Russel Wallace**, had come up with a similar idea at almost the same time! This competition pushed Darwin to share his work with the world. The theory of Darwin became one of the most important ideas in biology, helping us understand the incredible diversity of life on our planet.

69. **Marie Curie** was one of the most important scientists of all time. In 1898, working alongside her husband, she discovered **two new elements: radium and polonium**. Marie won the Nobel Prize twice: in physics(1903) and chemistry (1911). She was the first woman who had ever done that. In the early days of research into radioactivity, scientists did not fully understand the risks of radiation. Marie Curie worked extensively with radioactive substances, even carrying samples in her pockets. Unfortunately, this work had serious consequences for her health.

70. **The first working laser** was invented **in 1960** by an American scientist named **Theodore Maiman**. He used a ruby crystal to create this remarkable beam of light, which differed from regular light because it was all one color and traveled in a very narrow beam. People use lasers for lots of different things. You see them in **barcode scanners** at stores, in **laser printers** that print your homework, and even in laser surgery, where doctors use them to carefully remove tissue or fix vision. They are also essential for **sending information** through **fiber optic cables**, which are like tiny glass wires that carry light signals.

1.9. Materials and Technologies

71. Plastic is everywhere today, but it has not always been around. One of the first steps toward the plastics we know today happened **in 1855**, when a British scientist named **Alexander Parkes** invented **celluloid**, the first synthetic plastic. He used cellulose, a plant-based material, to create this new substance.

People used celluloid to make jewelry, toys, buttons, and other things. While celluloid was an important early plastic, it was not exactly like the plastics we use now, and it did not become super popular right away. However, it set the stage for many other plastic inventions to come.

72. **The next big step** in the story of plastic came **in 1907** when a Belgian chemist named **Leo Baekeland** invented **Bakelite**. Bakelite was much simpler to make in large quantities, which made it much cheaper. This ease of production allowed for the mass production of plastic materials, leading to their widespread adoption in various industries, notably electronics and cars.

73. In the middle of the 20th century, around the 1930s and 1940s, scientists started making many **new types of plastic**. One important discovery was polyethylene **in 1933**. This is the material used to make those plastic grocery bags and the containers you keep food in. Then, **in 1935**, the **DuPont** company invented **nylon**. People use it in everything from stockings to toothbrushes, and **teflon**, which makes your frying pan non-stick.

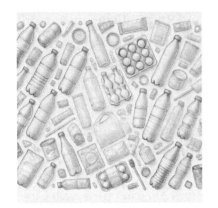

74. Plastic is widely used for packaging. That is because plastic is super useful for keeping things safe and fresh. It is light, so it does not add much weight to what one carries. It is waterproof, so it keeps liquids in and moisture out and lasts a long time. That is why we see so much plastic used for packaging food, drinks, and almost everything else we buy at the store. About 40% of all the packaging we use consists of plastic.

75. Plastic is also crucial in medicine. Disposable syringes, for instance, are made from plastic and are intended for single use, minimizing the risk of infection. Plastic also makes sterile packaging that keeps bandages and other medical supplies clean and safe. Even implants, which are placed inside the body, are often made of special types of plastic. Because of plastic, medical procedures are much safer and cleaner than they used to be.

76. Although plastic is useful in many ways, it does cause some **big problems for the environment**. Unlike food scraps or paper, plastic **does not decompose**, meaning it does not rot or break down naturally. Billions of tons of plastic waste end up in landfills, oceans, and other places in nature. Scientists and engineers are working on **new ways to recycle plastic** and to create new materials that will decompose naturally, helping to solve this huge problem.

77. Richard Feynman (1918–1988), an American physicist and Nobel Prize winner, is considered one of the first scientists to consider **nanotechnology**. In a famous speech, **"There is Plenty of Room at the Bottom,"** he gave in 1959, Feynman suggested that we could learn to control matter at the tiniest level: **the level of molecules and atoms.** He imagined a future where we could precisely **control individual atoms and molecules** to engineer materials with unprecedented properties. This speech was like a spark that helped ignite the field of nanotechnology.

78. Nanotechnology is revolutionizing **modern medicine**, particularly in treating diseases like cancer. Scientists are developing a new way to deliver medicine that is much more precise. They use tiny particles called **nanoparticles** to carry the medicine directly to the cells that need it, like cancer cells. Such treatment minimizes damage to healthy tissues and reduces adverse side effects associated with traditional chemotherapy. Nanotechnology is also helping to make **super-efficient solar panels**. **Tiny particles of silver** help the solar panels soak up more sunlight and convert it into electricity much more effectively, making them way more powerful.

79. Nanotechnology is also helping to make **super-efficient solar panels**. **Tiny particles of silver** help the solar panels soak up more sunlight and convert it into electricity much more effectively, making them way more powerful.

80. Nanoparticles are commonly used in **cosmetics,** especially sunscreens. **Sunscreens** often contain mineral ingredients like **titanium oxide and zinc oxide to provide UV protection**, and in the past sunscreens left a white, pasty film on the skin because the particles that block the sun were too big. However, now scientists can make these particles much smaller, so tiny they become invisible without losing their effectiveness. This technology makes the sunscreen much nicer to use, providing great protection from sunburn.

81. Think about how heavy metal is. Imagine something as strong as metal but much, much lighter. That is what scientists are creating for airplanes and spaceships using nanotechnology. For example, scientists use tiny tubes made of carbon, called **carbon nanotubes**, to create **new materials** that are 5 to 10 times lighter and stronger than steel! It makes a huge difference for airplanes and rockets because lighter vehicles can fly higher and faster and use much less fuel.

82. Nanotechnology helps make clothes that stay **dry and clean**. Scientists use nanoparticles of **silver or titanium dioxide** to coat fabrics. This method creates a protective barrier against water and dirt. Such fabrics are used in special **antibacterial clothes** that help prevent germs from growing, in **leather jackets** to keep them from getting water spots, and in **sportswear** that keeps you dry even when you exercise hard. These clothes are also much easier to clean!

83. **Stainless steel** was invented **in 1913** by **Harry Brearley,** a British metallurgist. Brearley created a type of steel that does not rust because he added a lot of **chromium** (more than 10%) to it. Rust happens when iron in steel reacts with air and water, but the chromium acts like a shield, preventing this from happening.

84. Before stainless steel, **people produced kitchen tools** and **medical instruments** of regular steel or other metals. However, these materials could rust or react with cleaning chemicals. **In the 1930s,** people started using stainless steel more and more because it did not have these problems.

This steel was much stronger than other metals, lasted much longer, and could easily be cleaned without getting damaged by acids or other cleaning stuff.

85. The story of stainless steel did not end there. Scientists discovered that adding another metal called **nickel** could make it even more amazing. Nickel made **stainless steel** more **flexible** and **able to withstand strong impacts**, so it would not crack or break easily when bent or hit. It was a significant improvement because it meant stainless steel could be used to build much bigger and stronger things like skyscrapers, cars, and even the fastest airplanes. This method opened up many new possibilities for using stainless steel in different industries.

86. In the 1970s, Japanese scientists developed new versions of stainless steel, including what they called "**super stainless steel.**" It could withstand even the harshest conditions, like salty ocean water and the chemicals used in the oil industry. Now you can find this super strong stainless steel in ships, oil platforms at sea, and even the pipes that carry oil underwater.

2.Space
2.1. The Moon

87. How was the Moon formed?
Scientists think the Moon was formed a long time ago, about 4.5 billion years ago, when a planet about the size of Mars, nicknamed Theia, smashed into the Earth. The impact was so powerful that it sent chunks of Earth and Theia flying into space.

These chunks formed a ring of debris around Earth. Over millions of years, gravity pulled them together to create our natural satellite. This idea explains why it consists of similar stuff to Earth and why Earth is tilted a little bit on its side.

88. The Moon does not make its light. It reflects light from the Sun. Sunlight travels millions of miles to reach the Moon, and when it hits its surface, some of that light bounces back toward Earth, making it shine in our night sky. As the Moon travels around Earth, different parts of it are lit up by the Sun, creating the different phases we see. When the whole side facing us is illuminated, it is a full moon. When the side facing us is in shadow, it is a new moon.

89.The Moon is always on the move, orbiting Earth. Like Earth, half of it is always illuminated by the Sun, but because the Moon spins at the same rate it orbits us, we only see one side. As the Moon travels around us, we see different amounts of the lit-up side. That is why we see the Moon change shape, going through phases like a new moon (when it seems to disappear), a first quarter (when it is half full), a full moon (when it is a bright circle), and a last quarter (when the other half is lit). This entire cycle takes about **29.5 days.**

90. A full moon happens when the Earth is right between the Sun and the Moon, and the whole side of the satellite that faces us is lit up. It occurs about every 29.5 days. Here is a fun fact: There are usually 12 full moons a year, but sometimes there are 13! When this happens, the extra one is called a **"Blue Moon."** The name has to do with how rare it is, not the color of the Moon.

91.The Moon's surface has dents and holes called **craters**. These **giant holes** were formed long ago when meteorites and asteroids smashed into the Moon. The Moon does not have a thick atmosphere like Earth, which means there is nothing to protect its surface from these impacts. So, when a meteorite or asteroid hits the Moon, it leaves a big mark that stays there.

92. One of the largest craters on the Moon is called **the South Pole-Aitken Basin**. It is about 1,600 miles wide. Because the Moon does not have wind or rain like Earth, these craters stay the same for billions of years. They are like a record of what happened in the early solar system.

2.2. Planets of the Solar System

93. Our solar system has eight planets: Earth, Mercury, Venus, Mars, Jupiter, Saturn, Uranus, and Neptune. Besides the planets, there are also dwarf planets, moons, asteroids, comets, and space dust.

94. Pluto was considered the ninth planet in our solar system for a long time. But in 2006, astronomers changed their minds and reclassified Pluto as a dwarf planet.

95. All the **planets** in our solar system **travel around the Sun**. They move in their paths, called orbits, which keeps them from crashing into each other. And the gravity of the Sun keeps all the planets from flying away into space.

96. Imagine swinging a ball on a string. The path the ball makes is like an **orbit**. The ball is like a planet or a moon, and your hand is like the Sun or a planet. The string keeps the ball from flying away like gravity keeps planets and moons in their orbits. Because gravity pulls the objects together, the orbit is not a perfect circle; it is more of an oval shape.

97. The planets in our solar system are all different. Each planet is unique, with its size, what it consists of, and its conditions. Some planets have thick air, while others have almost none. Some are scorching hot, while others are cold. The four closest to the Sun — Mercury, Venus, Earth, and Mars — are known as terrestrial, rocky planets. They consist of hard rock and metal, like Earth, but they are much smaller than the other planets. The other four — Jupiter, Saturn, Uranus, and Neptune — are farther away from the Sun and are mainly composed of gases like hydrogen and helium.

98. Have you ever wondered where the names of the planets come from? The majority of them were named after **Roman gods and goddesses**. However, Roman mythology was very similar to Greek mythology, so many of those gods have Greek versions. Only **Uranus** is named directly after a Greek god. He was the god of the sky. The Romans did not have a matching god, so they used the Greek name. The other planets were named after Roman gods, but those gods were based on Greek gods:

- **Mercury** - the speedy messenger god, like the Greek Hermes
- **Venus** - the goddess of love and beauty, like the Greek Aphrodite
- **Mars** - the god of war, like the Greek Ares
- **Jupiter** - the king of the gods, like the Greek Zeus

- **Saturn** - the god of time, like the Greek Cronus
- **Neptune**- the god of the sea, like the Greek Poseidon

So, even though most of the planet names are Roman, the connection to Greek mythology is clear.

99. The largest gas giants are Jupiter and Saturn.

100. Earth is a pretty special place! So far, it is **the only planet we know of in our solar system that can support life.** The other planets are just too extreme. Some are scorching hot, like Mercury, where you would instantly burn up. Others are cold, like Neptune, where you would instantly freeze. The air on some planets is full of poisonous gases that we cannot breathe, and the surfaces of other planets are either like bubbling hot soup or dry, cracked deserts.

101. On some planets (Mars, Uranus, Neptune) there is **water,** but it is **frozen.**

2.3. Mercury, Venus, and Mars

102. Which planet is closest to the Sun? It is **Mercury**! Mercury is a little bit bigger than our Moon. Its surface is rocky and bumpy, just like the Moon. It has mountains, flat areas, cliffs, and craters of all different sizes. The largest crater on Mercury, Caloris Planitia, spans 963 miles in width.

103. On Earth, it takes 365 days to go around the Sun, which is one year. But Mercury is much closer to the Sun, so it has the shortest orbital period of all the planets in our solar system and goes around much faster! **A year on Mercury is only about 89 Earth days.**

104. The planet **Mercury** got its name from **the ancient Roman god Mercury**, the speedy messenger of the gods.

105. You might think Mercury is **the hottest planet** since it is closest to the Sun, but you would be wrong! The hottest planet is **Venus**! Venus has a super thick atmosphere that acts like a giant blanket, trapping heat from the Sun. This is called the greenhouse effect, and it is super strong on Venus. It makes the surface incredibly hot, around 900 degrees Fahrenheit, which is hot enough to melt lead.

106. Venus and Mercury have no satellites.

107. Venus zooms around the Sun in about 225 Earth days, which equals the length of a Venusian year. But spinning on its axis is a much slower process. It takes Venus about 243 Earth days to complete one rotation, which equals a Venusian day. So, **on Venus, a day is longer than a year!**

108. Which planet is called Earth's sister? It is Venus! It is very similar to Earth in size and mass. However, Venus is entirely covered by a thick layer of clouds made of sulfuric acid, a strong and dangerous acid! These clouds are so thick that they block most of the sunlight, making the surface of Venus a dim and gloomy place. There are also winds on Venus, but they are not as strong as the winds on Earth.

109. Why is **Mars** red? The surface of Mars is covered in **rusty-colored dust**. This dust contains a lot of **iron oxide**, the same compound that makes rust on Earth. This compound is reddish. That is why Mars is often called the **Red Planet**.

110. Mars has ice at its north and south poles. This ice melts and freezes depending on the time of year.

111. We know a lot about our home planet, Earth, but **which planet have we explored the most?** That would be **Mars**! We have sent many robots, called rovers, to drive around on Mars and study its rocks and air. It is like Mars has its team of space explorers! In 2020, it was like a party on the way to Mars, with spacecraft from the United States, China, and the United Arab Emirates all launching missions almost simultaneously!

112. The tallest mountain in the entire solar system is on **Mars**! It is called **Olympus Mons**, and it is a giant volcano that is no longer active. It reaches a staggering height of 16.77 miles!

113. A day on Mars is slightly longer than a day on Earth, just a bit more than 24 hours. But **a year on Mars** is much longer than a year on Earth. It takes Mars about 687 Earth days to go around the Sun.

114. Mars has two moons, **Phobos and Deimos**. They are not round like our Moon; they look more like lumpy potatoes! Scientists believe these moons are asteroids that were pulled in by Mars's gravity.

2.4. Jupiter, Saturn, Uranus

115. Which planet has the shortest day in our solar system? It is **Jupiter!** A day on Jupiter is only about 10 hours long. That means Jupiter spins incredibly quickly. Jupiter is also the largest and heaviest planet. It is so massive that if you combined all the other planets, they would only weigh about half as much as Jupiter!

116. A year on Jupiter is very long, almost 12 Earth years. Jupiter has 95 moons. Jupiter also has three rings around it, made of tiny pieces of rock and dust. They are so difficult to see from Earth that we only discovered them when spacecraft flew nearby.

117. Jupiter has a giant red spot called the **Great Red Spot**. It is like an enormous hurricane, far bigger than any hurricane on Earth. It has been swirling in Jupiter's atmosphere for at least 350 years! The winds inside this giant storm are highly intense: their speed is around 430 miles per hour. Scientists think its red color comes from chemicals in Jupiter's atmosphere that react to sunlight. They are still trying to figure out why this storm has lasted so long.

118. Imagine waiting almost 30 Earth years for your next birthday! That is how long a year is on **Saturn - 29.5 Earth years**. But a day on Saturn is very short—only about 10 hours and 32 minutes! **Saturn's rings** are like a giant, shimmering hula hoop made of billions of tiny ice crystals, dust, and rocks. They are so bright that you can see them from Earth with a telescope. But every 15 years, these rings disappear! It happens because Saturn tilts, and we see the rings from the side, making them look thin and almost invisible.

119. Saturn has a big **group of moons:** there are **146** of them! The most famous of these moons is Titan. Titan is unique, as it has its air like a tiny planet! It is even larger than Mercury. **Saturn** itself is **a gas giant**, mostly made of helium and hydrogen.

120. Why is Uranus blue-green? Its atmosphere consists of gases like methane, hydrogen, and helium. The methane gas absorbs the red and yellow parts of sunlight and reflects the blue-green parts. That is why Uranus looks blue-green to us.

121. You might think the farthest planet from the Sun would be the coldest, but that is not the case! **The coldest planet in our solar system is Uranus!** It gets unbelievably cold there, around **-371** degrees Fahrenheit! Unlike the other gas giants, Uranus does not give off much heat from inside, which explains why it is so cold. Scientists are not entirely sure why, but they have some guesses. One idea is that Uranus is tilted on its side like it is rolling through space. Another idea is that something huge crashed into Uranus long ago, removing much of its internal heat. Whatever the reason, Uranus is the coldest of the giant planets.

122. All the other planets are like spinning tops that spin upright, but **Uranus** is like a top that has been knocked over and **is spinning on its side!** Scientists believe this strange tilt happened billions of years ago when Uranus collided with an enormous space rock. It takes Uranus **84 Earth years** to go around the Sun once. But a day on Uranus is much shorter, only about **17 hours.**

123. Which planet **in our solar system** has the year with the greatest duration? It is **Neptune!** A year on Neptune takes almost 165 Earth years.

124. Neptune has seasons, like Earth, but each season lasts about 40 Earth years. **Neptune's clouds** do not consist of water like Earth's clouds; they contain tiny crystals of frozen methane. These icy clouds are driven by winds that are so strong they are the fastest in the entire solar system, **up to 1,200 miles per hour!** These super-fast winds are caused by huge temperature differences between the cold outer atmosphere and the heat from inside Neptune. It makes Neptune's atmosphere one of the wildest and most extreme in our solar system.

2.5. Dwarf Planets

125. Dwarf planets are objects in space that orbit the Sun and are big enough to be round or almost round. But unlike regular planets, they have not cleared their orbital path of other objects like asteroids.

126. In 2006, astronomers from all over the world got together at a meeting called the International Astronomical Union and introduced a new category for space objects: **dwarf planets**. They decided that to be a regular planet, a space object has to meet three rules:

1) It **orbits the Sun.**
2) It is **big enough** to be nearly **round.**
3) It has **cleared its orbit** of other objects.

Dwarf planets pass the first two tests, but they fail the third. They share their orbital space with other objects like asteroids and icy rocks. So, dwarf planets represent a middle ground between full-sized planets and smaller objects like asteroids.

127. It can be tricky to keep track of all these space objects! **Pluto** used to be known as **the ninth planet** in our solar system, but in 2006, scientists changed its status to **a dwarf planet**. On the other hand, **Ceres**, which orbits between Mars and Jupiter, used to be called an asteroid, but now it is also classified as a dwarf planet.

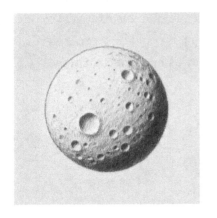

128. The officially recognized dwarf planets in our solar system are:

- **Pluto:** The most famous dwarf planet, located in the Kuiper Belt. It has five moons, the largest of which is Charon.
- **Ceres:** The only dwarf planet in the main asteroid belt between Mars and Jupiter. It was the first dwarf planet to be discovered.

- **Eris:** It is about the same mass as Pluto but slightly smaller in size and is located beyond Pluto's orbit.
- **Haumea:** An object in the Kuiper Belt known for its unusual egg shape and fast spin.
- **Makemake:** Also found in the Kuiper Belt, it has a very bright, icy surface.

129. These dwarf planets help scientists understand how our solar system formed and changed over time. What are **dwarf planets** made of? They are like **a mix of rock and different kinds of ice**, including water ice (like the ice in your freezer), methane ice (a type of gas that is frozen solid), and even nitrogen ice (which is super cold!). They are not moons of other planets, although some dwarf planets may even have oceans hidden beneath their icy surfaces, like Pluto.

130. Scientists think there could be many more dwarf planets hiding out in our solar system that we have not discovered yet! One of the first dwarf planets we found was **Ceres**. It was discovered **in 1801** by an Italian astronomer named Giuseppe Piazzi. He named it after Ceres, the Roman goddess of agriculture and harvest.

131. Ceres has no satellites.

132. So, which **dwarf planet is the smallest**? It is **Ceres**! Its diameter is only about 590 miles. Ceres has ice and minerals, and it is relatively close to Earth. Because of this, some scientists think it could be a good place for future space missions to stop on their way to farther destinations.

2.6. Small Bodies of the Solar System

133. Our solar system is more than just made of planets and moons; it also has **small bodies of the solar system**. These include comets, asteroids, and meteoroids. Even though they are smaller than planets, they play a big role in shaping our solar system. When they crash into planets or moons, they leave behind big holes called craters. Sometimes, planets even capture them and turn them into moons.

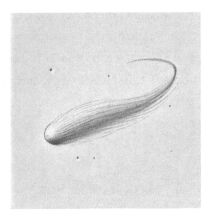

134. Comets are like giant, dirty snowballs from space! They are composed of ice, dust, frozen gases, and little bits of rock. Comets travel around the Sun in a very stretched-out oval shape, like if you took a circle and pulled on both ends.

135. When a comet gets closer and closer to the Sun, things start to happen! The Sun's heat warms up the comet's icy center, the **nucleus**. The ice and frozen gases begin to evaporate, turning into a glowing, fuzzy cloud around it. This cloud is called the coma. The Sun's wind and light push gas and dust away from the coma, creating **a long, beautiful tail**.

136. A comet has two tails: a gas tail and a dust one. **The gas tail** always points directly away from the Sun because of the solar wind. **The dust tail** is more curved and follows the path of the comet.

137. **As a comet moves away from the Sun**, it cools down, and its core starts to freeze again. The ice stops turning into gas, and the tail and coma disappear. It becomes "dormant," or inactive.

138. A comet can make this trip around the Sun many times, getting closer and farther away. Each time it gets close to the Sun, some amount of its ice evaporates. Eventually, after many trips, all the ice is used up. Then, the **comet loses its coma and tail and becomes a dark, rocky object that looks like an asteroid.**

139. Comets might look big and bright in the sky, but their solid centers, called **nuclei**, are usually small, only about **1 to 10 miles** across. However, some are much larger! Comet **Hale-Bopp**, for example, had a nucleus of about **37 miles** across. When a comet gets close to the Sun, it heats up and forms a huge, fuzzy cloud called a **coma**. This coma can expand to be **60,000** miles across or even more. And the comet's **tails**, made of gas and dust, can stretch for **millions of miles**. So, even though its nucleus is small, its atmosphere and tail can become unbelievably huge when it gets close to the Sun.

140. **Halley's Comet** is the most famous of all comets. It comes back to Earth's neighborhood about every 75–76 years. Its nucleus is about 9 miles long. We last saw it in 1986, and it will return in 2061.

141. **Asteroids are rocky, irregularly shaped bodies** that orbit the Sun. They are significantly smaller than planets and categorized as small solar system bodies. The majority of known asteroids are found in the main asteroid belt, a region between the orbits of Mars and Jupiter.

142. Scientists have a strong theory that a massive asteroid struck Earth about 65 million years ago, and this event led to the extinction of the dinosaurs, along with many other plants and animals. The crash created a huge crater called Chicxulub in present-day Mexico.

143. Long ago, some scientists thought that the **asteroid belt between Mars and Jupiter** was the remains of a destroyed planet. But today, most scientists believe it is the opposite: it consists of pieces of a planet that never quite formed.

144. A meteoroid is a small, rocky, or metallic object that travels through space. When a meteoroid gets pulled into Earth's atmosphere, it rubs against the air and gets super hot. This effect makes it glow brightly, creating a beautiful streak of light across the night sky. That is a **meteor**, also known as a shooting star. If any part of the meteoroid survives the trip and hits the ground, it is called a **meteorite**.

145. What is the difference between an asteroid and a meteoroid? It is mostly about size and where they started their journey. **Asteroids** are bigger, up to hundreds of miles across, and they orbit the Sun. **Meteoroids** are much smaller, from specks of dust to rocks a few feet wide. They are often pieces that have broken off from asteroids or comets.

146. Have you ever seen a shooting star? That is what it looks like when a meteoroid falls to Earth! Meteoroids zoom through space at incredible speeds, but as they enter Earth's atmosphere, it is like hitting a giant air cushion. The friction from the air makes them heat up so much that they glow brightly, creating a beautiful streak of light across the night sky.

147. When a large meteorite crashes into Earth, it creates a big hole called an **astrobleme**. The word "astrobleme" comes from Greek words that mean "star wound," a pretty cool name for a scar left by a space rock! The biggest astroblemes appeared millions of years ago when Earth was bombarded by huge meteorites.

148. Even giant craters do not last forever. Wind, rain, and volcanic activity slowly wear them down over millions of years. A great example of this is the **Manicouagan** Crater in Canada. The lower part of this ancient crater is now filled with water, creating a beautiful ring-shaped lake called the **Manicouagan Reservoir.**

149. **The biggest crater on Earth is the Vredefort Crater** in South Africa. This crater is the biggest impact scar we know of on Earth. It is about 300 kilometers across. It is hard to imagine how enormous the space rock must have been to make such a giant hole!
In 2005, **the Vredefort Crater** was declared a UNESCO World Heritage Site.

150. In 2005, **the Vredefort Crater** was declared a UNESCO World Heritage Site.

2.7. Astronomical Phenomena

151. Every now and then, Earth passes through a swarm of meteorites, and we see **a large number of shooting stars at the same time**. This spectacular event is called a **meteorite shower**.

152. Have you ever imagined all the planets lining up in space? That is what **a planet parade** is! All the planets orbit the Sun, each on its path. Sometimes, they all happen to be on the same side of the Sun, and from our view of Earth, they look like they stand in a line. The last full planet parade happened in 1982.

153. **What is an eclipse?** It is when one object in space blocks the light from another or when one object passes into the shadow of another. When the Moon moves between the Earth and the Sun, it blocks the Sun's light, causing a solar eclipse. If the Moon completely covers the Sun, it gets dark, even in the daytime! And sometimes, during a total solar eclipse, you can see amazing flames of fire shooting out from around the dark circle of the Moon. These flames are called prominences.

154. **A partial solar eclipse** happens when the Moon does not completely cover the Sun.

155. **A lunar eclipse** occurs when the Earth passes between the Sun and the Moon, casting its shadow on the Moon. This phenomenon can only happen during a full moon when the Sun, Earth, and Moon are aligned. During a total lunar eclipse, the Moon can turn a beautiful reddish color. It happens because some sunlight bends around the Earth and through its atmosphere, and this bent light makes the Moon look red.

156. Have you ever seen a neon sign? It glows because electricity passes through gases. **The Northern Lights** are like a giant neon sign in the sky! Tiny particles from the Sun act like electricity, and the gases in Earth's atmosphere act like the gases in the sign. When the particles hit the gases, they make the sky glow with beautiful colors like green, pink, and purple. You are most likely to see this beautiful light show near the North Pole in places like Alaska or Norway.

157. Have you ever seen a shooting star? Imagine seeing lots of them all at once! That is what **a meteor shower** is like. When a comet travels close to Earth, it leaves a trail of tiny pieces of ice and space dust. These pieces are all moving together in the same direction.

As Earth orbits the Sun, it sometimes passes through this trail of comet debris. When this happens, the tiny pieces enter our atmosphere and burn up, creating a dazzling display of light, a meteor shower. It looks like stars are raining down from the sky.

158. Meteors travel about 200 times faster than the fastest airplanes. That is why it does not make sense to try to watch them with a telescope. Instead, scientists and photographers use high-speed cameras to capture these bright light streaks.

159. Do meteor showers have names? Yes! Meteor showers happen at certain times of the year and appear in specific parts of the sky. So, they are named after the constellations they seem to come from. For example, a shower that appears in the area of the Leo constellation is called the Leonids, and a shower in the area of the Lyra constellation is called the Lyrids.

2.8. Outside the Solar System

160. Just like our Sun has planets orbiting it, other stars out in space have their own families of planets! These planets that orbit other stars are called **exoplanets**. It is like each star has its little solar system, and we are just one of many.

161. Many of the **exoplanets** discovered by scientists are **giant balls of gas**, just like Jupiter in our solar system. These gas giants do not have a hard, rocky surface to walk on. If you tried to land on one, you would sink into the thick gases!

162. Scientists have discovered thousands of **exoplanets**, but they still do not know if there is life on even one of them.

163. **What is a galaxy?** Stars might look scattered randomly across the sky, but they are not! They are held together by gravity, forming huge groups called galaxies.

164. Each **galaxy** has stars, planets, star clusters, and dusty nebulas.

165. **You might think all stars are the same as our Sun,** but that is not true! Stars are very different from each other. They come in different sizes, some much bigger and some much smaller than the Sun. They also have different masses, colors, and temperatures.

166. When we look up at the night sky, most stars seem to be white, but that is an illusion. **A star's actual color depends on how hot it is.** The hottest stars are blue or white. Stars that are a bit cooler appear orange or red. And just like Earth spins on its axis, all stars spin too, but some spin much faster than others.

167. The distances from our solar system to other stars are so huge that scientists use a special measurement called a **"light-year."** A light-year is the distance light travels in one year. That is about **5.88 trillion miles!** It is not a measurement of time, but a way to measure enormous distances in space. For example, the closest star to us, Proxima Centauri, is about **4.24 light-years** away.

168. Have you ever wondered **how stars are born?** In space, there are huge clouds of dust and gas. Gravity, the force that keeps you on the ground, makes these clouds bump into each other, and the stuff inside starts to compress. As the clouds get squeezed tighter and tighter, they get hotter and hotter. Eventually, the center of the cloud becomes a hot, dense ball called a protostar. It is like a baby star. When the temperature in the core reaches about **18 million degrees Fahrenheit** nuclear reactions begin. This is like a giant explosion inside the star, and it is what makes the star shine brightly. This whole process of star birth can take millions of years.

169. **There is a constant battle happening inside every star!** Gravity constantly pulls all the gas inward, squeezing it toward the center. But at the same time, the incredible heat and pressure in the star's core are pushing outward with a powerful force. It is quite a delicate balance.

170. **How do stars change over time?** When a star like our Sun runs out of hydrogen fuel in its core, it expands enormously, becoming a red giant. These red giants are so huge that they can swallow up anything in its path. Over time, the red giant cools down, shrinks, and becomes a white dwarf.

171. What are black holes? In space, there are places with very strong gravity. They are like super-powerful vacuum cleaners, sucking in everything around them. Nothing can escape, not even light (the fastest thing in the universe). These objects are called black holes.

172. How did scientists find black holes? For a long time, scientists thought black holes existed. They could not see them with telescopes because black holes do not give off light or other radiation like X-rays or radio waves. But even though we cannot see black holes directly, they **affect nearby celestial bodies through their gravity**, and this is how scientists finally discovered them.

173. It took a long time, but scientists finally captured **the first-ever photograph** of a black hole! It happened **in 2019** using the **Event Horizon Telescope (EHT)**. The picture shows the dark shadow of a supermassive black hole at the center of a galaxy called **M87, 55 million light-years** away from us.

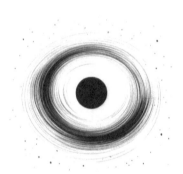

174. A black hole can swallow a whole planet if the planet gets too close. But do not worry! There are no black holes near our solar system, so Earth is perfectly safe.

175. What are supernovas? The biggest stars can undergo rapid explosion and then slowly fade away. It is a massive explosion that happens when the most massive stars reach the end of their lives. This exploding star is called a supernova. For a few weeks or months, a supernova shines incredibly brightly, sometimes even brighter than all the other stars in its galaxy combined! It is not visible from Earth during the daytime.

176. A star can only become a supernova once. After the explosion, most of the star's material is blasted out into space, spreading its parts across the universe.

177. We cannot predict when a star will become a supernova. But people have witnessed these incredible explosions throughout history. **The first record of a supernova** is from Chinese writings **in the year 185**. And **in 1054**, Chinese astronomers spotted a supernova that was brighter than Venus.

178. What is a nebula? After a supernova explosion, a huge cloud of dust and gases (like hydrogen, helium, and others) forms. This is a nebula. This cloud reflects the light from nearby stars, making it look like a glowing, colorful patch in the sky. Nebulas can shine in reds, blues, greens, and other colors. It will take millions of years for new stars to be born from these nebulas.

179. The Crab Nebula was created by a supernova explosion in the year 1054.

180. Nebulas have amazing shapes. Some look like a horse's head, a cat's eye, a rose, and so on.

181. Are there any stars brighter than the Sun? Yes, definitely! Some stars shine much brighter, while others are dimmer. However, a dimmer star can appear just as bright as a brighter star if it is closer to us. It is all about how far away they are.

182. Arcturus is a giant star that is much bigger and brighter than our Sun. It shines 170 times brighter and is 25 times larger.

183. Our Sun is crucial to us, although it is not the biggest star. **Many stars are much larger.** To tell the truth, the Sun is a pretty average star in the universe. For example, **the blue star Rigel is 62 times bigger than the Sun.** And get this: there are even stars that are thousands of times bigger than Rigel.

184. Some of the biggest stars can be seen in the night sky, like **Mu Cephei** and **Betelgeuse**. These are red **supergiants**, incredibly huge stars. If the smaller one, Betelgeuse, replaced our Sun, its surface would reach Jupiter's orbit.

185. Which star is the brightest? It is **Sirius**! But it is so far away that the Moon and Venus sometimes look brighter to us. And Sirius is not just one star; it is a pair of stars orbiting each other! There is a bright, bluish-white star and a much smaller, dimmer star called a white dwarf.

186. How long would it take to travel to the nearest star? Our closest stellar neighbor is the Alpha Centauri system. In the night sky, it appears as one bright star, much like Sirius. But do not be fooled! Alpha Centauri is a triple star system, meaning it consists of three stars: Alpha Centauri A, Alpha Centauri B, and Proxima Centauri, also known as Alpha Centauri C. Of the three, Proxima Centauri is the closest to us, and it is 4.3 light-years away.

187. Alpha Centauri can be seen in the night sky from the Southern Hemisphere.

188. With our current spaceships, it would take **tens of thousands of years** to travel to **Proxima Centauri**.

189. Could there be life on planets in the Alpha Centauri system? In 2016, scientists found an exoplanet circling Proxima Centauri and named it Proxima B. They believe Proxima B might be home to life because it orbits its star in a zone where living things could theoretically survive. Proxima b is also almost the same size as Earth.

190. The North Star is located directly above the North Pole, so long ago, when people saw it in the night sky, they knew where the north was.

191. Like Sirius and Alpha Centauri, **the North Star** is not just one star. It is a system of stars that look like a single point of light to us.

192. What are binary stars? It is when two stars are close enough to be pulled together by gravity. They orbit each other like dancers. Scientists believe that about half of all stars in our Milky Way galaxy belong to a binary system.

2.9. Constellations

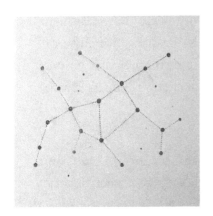

193. What is a constellation? People imagined connecting groups of bright stars with imaginary lines to create pictures of animals, birds, and heroes from myths and legends. These star pictures are called constellations. Long ago, sailors used constellations like maps to navigate the seas.

194. There are **88 constellations** in the sky, visible from both the Northern and Southern Hemispheres.

195. In the Northern Hemisphere, the most well-known constellations are **Ursa Major** (the Great Bear) and **Cygnus** (the Swan).

196. Who came up with the names for the constellations? Most of them came to us from the ancient Greeks. Although some may have originated with even older civilizations, like the Sumerians. As telescopes developed in the 15th through 18th centuries, European astronomers discovered fainter stars and created names for new constellations.

197. An astronomer named Claudius Ptolemy, who lived in the 2nd century, wrote about **48 constellations** in his books.

198. Betelgeuse is part of the constellation Orion, and **the North Star** belongs to the constellation Ursa Minor (the Little Bear).

2.10. Galaxies

199. Our galaxy has a cool name: the Milky Way! On a clear night, you can sometimes see it stretching across the sky like a hazy river of light. It looks like a band of closely packed stars. But here is the thing: those stars that seem so close together are incredibly far apart in space.

200. Our galaxy, like other galaxies, **spins around** its center.

201. Galaxies are grouped into **four main types** based on their shape:

- **Spiral galaxies:** These have a flat disk with a bright center and spiral arms. Our galaxy, the **Milky Way,** is a spiral galaxy.
- **Elliptical galaxies:** These range in shape from almost round to stretched out like a football. They mostly consist of older stars.
- **Lenticular galaxies:** These are like a mix between spiral and elliptical galaxies. They have a central bulge and a disk, but they do not have spiral arms.
- **Irregular galaxies:** These do not have a regular shape at all. They often consist of young stars, gas, and dust. **The Large Magellanic Cloud** is an example of an irregular galaxy.

These types were first classified by astronomer Edwin Hubble in 1926.

202. Galaxies are constantly on the move, and they do so **in two main ways.** First, they are pulled towards each other by gravity and orbit within groups called galaxy clusters. Second, they are moving away from each other because the universe is expanding. The farther away a galaxy is, the faster it is moving away. This is proof that the universe is still getting bigger.

203. Some galaxies can shoot out streams of hot gas and tiny particles across space for millions of light-years. These powerful blasts come from the center of the galaxy, where a supermassive black hole is located. For example, the galaxy **Messier 87 (M87)** has a jet that extends for more than **5,000 light-years.** These jets are like cosmic delivery trucks, carrying energy and materials across the universe.

3. Games

3.1. Ancient Games

204. People have been playing games for a long time, and one of the oldest board games we know about is called **Senet**. It is over **5,000 years old**! It was popular in Ancient Egypt, and even pharaohs like Tutankhamun played it. Senet was found in tombs, as people believed it helped the player travel to the afterlife.

205. Imagine a mix of soccer, basketball, and a bit of ancient ritual all rolled into one! This is like the **Mesoamerican ballgame**, one of the oldest sports in the world, dating back about **3,000** years. Played by pre-Columbian civilizations such as the Maya and Aztecs, the game involved propelling a solid rubber ball through a vertical stone ring using only the hips, elbows, knees, and all other body parts except the hands. It was not just a game to them; it was also like a religious ceremony.

206. Long ago **in Ancient Greece, people loved to play games**, and one of their favorites was called **petteia**. It was a bit like our modern game of checkers. Players moved small stones or pieces on a board, trying to outmaneuver their opponent and capture their game pieces. This game is often mentioned in ancient Greek writings, and both children and adults enjoyed playing it.

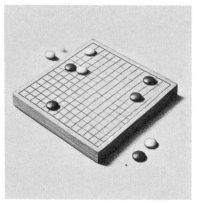

207. Over 2,500 years ago, a fascinating strategy game called Go was born in Ancient China. It is one of the oldest board strategy games still played today. The goal is simple but challenging: players take turns placing black and white stones on a grid-shaped board, trying to surround more territory than their opponent. In China, Go was considered a game for wise people and was an important part of cultural education.

208. In the game of **Go, there are so many possible moves** that the number is greater than the number of atoms in the entire universe. This complexity makes Go one of the most challenging strategy games.

209. During the Middle Ages in **Japan**, the game of **Go** was not just a pastime but a serious pursuit! The government supported **special schools** dedicated to teaching and mastering Go. These schools helped spread the popularity of the game. The best Go players, called Go masters, were highly respected and could even become advisors to the emperor, thanks to their amazing strategic minds.

210. Even after thousands of years, Go is still popular all over the world, especially in East Asian countries like **China, Japan**, and **South Korea**, where there is a professional system for players. These countries even have professional Go players who compete in major tournaments with prize money that can reach millions of dollars! It is amazing how an ancient game can still be that exciting and engaging today.

211. In Ancient India, one of the most popular games was **Chaturanga**, a game that is the ancestor of modern chess. It appeared around **the 6th century** and was a four-player strategy game. The pieces represented different parts of an army: foot soldiers, elephants, horses, and chariots. Chaturanga later spread to other countries and changed over time into the chess we play today.

212. Long before video games or even board games, people used dice. These little cubes have been around for a seriously long time. The first dice we know about were found in Mesopotamia and are about **5,000 years old**! Early dice consisted of animal bones. People in Ancient Egypt, Greece, and Rome used dice for both games and telling the future. Modern six-sided dice with numbered faces showed up around **1,000 BC** and have not changed much since then.

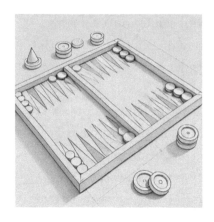

213. Backgammon is one of the oldest board games, dating back over **5,000 years**. Archaeologists have found backgammon boards in the tomb of the Egyptian pharaoh Tutankhamun and ancient digs in Mesopotamia. Backgammon is still super popular today because it is a fun mix of luck and strategy. You need to roll the dice, and you also need to be smart about how you move your pieces to win.

214. The Royal Game of Ur is one of the oldest board games, dating back over **4,500 years**. Game boards and pieces have been found in ancient tombs in the city of Ur, in Mesopotamia. The game combines strategy and luck and was historically played for fun and fortune-telling. Archaeologists have figured out the rules, so you can even play it today!

215. Mehen is an ancient Egyptian board game that is over **5,000 years old**. The game board looked like a coiled snake. Players moved lion-shaped pieces and balls around the sections of the spiral. Mehen was not just a game; it also had religious meaning. The snake symbolized protection for the sun and the pharaoh. The game disappeared around **2300 BC**, and we do not know all the rules.

216. Hounds and Jackals is an ancient Egyptian board game dating back to approximately **2000 BC**. The game board consisted of 58 holes into which playing pieces were inserted. Players competed by moving their pieces along the board, **aiming to be** the first to reach the finish. The pieces resembled dogs and jackals. Archaeologists have found these game boards in the tombs of pharaohs, which tells us that it was a popular game with important people. The only problem is, we do not know exactly how they played it. The rules are lost to time, like a secret code we cannot crack.

217. Ludus duodecim scriptorum, or **XII scripta** - was a popular game in Ancient Rome starting in the **1st century BC**. The name means "Game of Twelve Lines." It started way back in the 1st century BC. The game board had three rows of twelve spaces, and players moved their pieces along these lines based on dice rolls. The goal was to move all your pieces across the board and off before your opponent. Ludus duodecim scriptorum was enjoyed by people from all levels of Roman society.

218. Another popular game in Ancient Rome was **Latrunculi**, which means "game of soldiers." It was a strategy game similar to checkers or chess. The goal was to trap your opponent's pieces by surrounding them on two sides. The game board looked like a checkerboard, and the number of pieces could change. Roman soldiers loved this game because it helped them practice tactical thinking.

219. **Pachisi** is an ancient board game from India that is over **1,500 years** old. The goal is to move all your pieces around the board and into the center before the other players. Players used to throw cowrie shells instead of dice to decide how many spaces to move. The game board was shaped like a cross, and everyone loved playing it, from regular people to powerful rulers like Emperor Akbar. Pachisi was so popular that it is even mentioned in ancient books. This game is a relative of modern games like **Ludo** and **Parcheesi**.

220. **Chaupar** is a version of the ancient Indian game **Pachisi**. It was especially popular in medieval India and was considered a game for royalty. Chaupar has similar rules to Pachisi: the goal is to move all your pieces around the cross-shaped board and get them to the center before the other players. The difference is that instead of cowrie shells, Chaupar used dice, and the board could be made of cloth or decorated with jewels for royal courts. The game is mentioned in the epic poem the **Mahabharata,** where it is used in a key plot point about a rivalry between the Pandavas and Kauravas.

221. **Patolli** is an ancient board game from South America, popular with the Aztecs over **2,000 years ago**. Players used beans with markings instead of dice, and the game board was shaped like a cross. The goal was to be the first to get all your pieces around the board. Here is the cool part: players often bet valuable stuff on the game, like jewelry or food.

222. The rules for **Patolli** are a bit of a mystery. The Aztecs did not write down the rules; they taught them to each other by talking. After the Spanish conquered the Aztecs in **the 16th century**, many cultural traditions were lost or banned, including gambling games. Archaeologists have looked at what Spanish writers said about the game and studied pictures of ancient stuff to develop some ideas about how people might have played the game.

223. **Gomoku** (also known as **Five in a Row**) is an ancient strategy game that started in **China** about **4,000 years ago**. It is played on a board that looks like a Go board with **a 19x19 grid**. Two players take turns placing black and white stones, trying to be the first to get **five of their stones in a row**: horizontally, vertically, or diagonally.

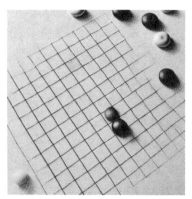

224. **Renju** is a strategy board game from **Japan** more than **a thousand years old**. It originates from the classic game **Gomoku**, where players take turns putting black and white stones on the lines of **a 15x15 grid**. The goal is to be the first to make a line of five of your stones.

225. **Renju** is like **Gomoku** but with a secret twist to make it even a distinctive variation. In Renju, the black player gets to go first, but they have extra restrictions to make the game fairer. Renju requires concentration and strategic thinking, so it is popular with people who like logic games.

226. Go and **Gomoku** are related, but only because they use the same **19x19** board and stones (black and white). They are very different games:

- **Go** is a strategy game where players capture territory by surrounding areas of the board with their stones. The goal is to control as much territory as possible.
- **Gomoku** is a logic game where the goal is to be the first to make a line of five stones in a row.

Even though the games look similar because of the board and stones, their rules and goals are completely different.

227. The Mill Game, or **Nine Men's Morris,** is an ancient board game that people played back in Roman times. Each player has nine pieces, and the goal is to make lines of three, called "mills," to capture your opponent's pieces. The player who leaves their opponent with less than three pieces wins.

228. The oldest **Nine Men's Morris** game board was found in Ancient Egypt, in the tomb of Pharaoh **Seti I**, dating back to about **the 13th century BC**. It shows that the game was known and popular long before it spread to Europe.

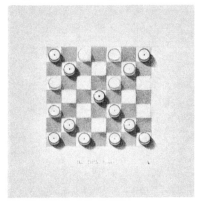

229. Checkers, a game with a rich history, dates back approximately **3,000 years**. The first checkerboards were discovered in **Egypt**, and they looked a bit like the checkerboards we use today, but they had fewer squares.

230. Get ready to learn about a game that has been around for over a thousand years! **Playing cards** were invented in **China** way back **in the 9th century**. But they were not always used for fun and games like we do today. People used them for games, of course, but also for fortune-telling and even betting. These early cards were not like the ones we use today. They were more like certain tiles or even pieces of paper money, and there were special rules for how to play.

231. **Dominoes** is an old board game that started in **China** around **the 12th century**. The first dominoes looked like dice and showed all the possible combinations you could roll with two dice.

3.2. Development and Distribution of Popular Games

232. In the 14th century, playing cards arrived in **Europe** through trade routes and the Crusaders. By this time, they had developed the suits we recognize today. The French suits we use now (spades, hearts, clubs, and diamonds) became the standard around the **1400s,** and after that, playing cards became popular worldwide.

233. In Europe, playing card suits were not just pictures; they stood for different groups of people in society:

- Hearts represented the church leaders and priests.
- Spades symbolized the brave knights and soldiers.
- Clubs stood for the farmers and peasants who worked the land.
- Diamonds represented clever merchants and traders.

234. In the 17th-19th centuries, with the invention of printing, the production of playing cards became widespread. Different deck styles appeared in England and Germany. At the same time, the kings and queens on the cards started to look like real people with distinctive characteristics.

235. In the 20th century, the **52-card deck** with four suits was standardized. Different games required different decks: poker, bridge, and solitaire.

236. During **the 18th century,** dominoes gained widespread popularity in **Europe,** particularly in France and Italy. The rules are simple: match the numbers on the ends of the tiles and try to be the first to play all your dominoes. Dominoes is still a favorite game for people of all ages.

237. The modern rules of checkers were developed in France in **the 15th century** when people started playing on an **8x8** checkerboard with 12 pieces per player. This new version of Checkers was a smash hit! It was easy enough for anyone to learn, but it also had enough strategy to keep players coming back for more. It was not long before checkers were being played all over Europe.

238. **Chaturanga**, a game of Indian origin dating back to approximately **the 6th century**, journeyed to Europe via **Persia** and **the Arab Caliphate**. In Persia, it transformed into a new game called **Shatranj**. Then, when the Arabs conquered Spain in the 8th and 9th centuries, Shatranj spread all over Europe.

239. **In Shatranj, the pieces had different names and moves**: the queen (vizier) could only move one square diagonally, and the bishop (al-fil) could move two squares diagonally, jumping over one square. The game was slower than modern chess.

240. **In the 11th century, Shatranj spread** to Spain, Italy, and France. The pieces got new names: the vizier became **the queen**, and the al-fil became **the bishop**. And the rules changed too, making the game even more exciting! Pawns got a super boost and could move two spaces on their first turn, and the queen and bishop became much more powerful.

241. In the 15th century, in Spain and Italy, the queen became the most powerful piece, able to move any number of squares horizontally, vertically, and diagonally. The bishop also got its modern move. These changes made the game faster and closer to modern chess.

242. Between the 15th and 17th centuries, chess started to look like the game we know and love today. Some new rules were added, like **castling**, a special move with the king and rook, and **en passant**, a tricky way to capture a pawn. This was also when people started having official chess tournaments. Chess became so popular with kings and queens that it earned the nickname "the game of kings," and it is still a favorite pastime of people all over the world.

243. The first official match for **the World Chess Championship** was held in 1886, with Wilhelm Steinitz as the winner.

244. In the Middle Ages, Nine Men's Morris was one of the most popular board games in Europe. It was frequently engraved on stone benches, wooden boards, and barrel lids. The game was valued not only as entertainment but also as a tool for developing strategic thinking. People of all social classes played it. The rules of the game are described in medieval texts.

245. Nine Men's Morris came to America with the first European settlers in **the 1600s and 1700s.** The colonists brought many popular board games, including Nine Men's Morris. This game quickly became a favorite pastime for families in the American colonies. It was a simple way to have fun and pass the time.

246. A game that became **the ancestor of modern checkers** first appeared **in France in the 12th century.** It was called **Fierges** and was played on a chessboard. This is when the basic rules of checkers began to take shape. Players could move their pieces one square diagonally, and if they could jump over an opponent's piece, they could capture it! It was the beginning of the checkers game we know and love today.

247. **In the 1400s,** checkers got a super cool new rule known as promotion, where a piece reaching the opposite side becomes a king. Kings are incredibly powerful, so they can move any number of squares, making the game more strategic and exciting.

248. In **the 20th century, the rules for international checkers** were standardized, and regular championships began.

249. The first official World Championship for international checkers took place **in 1894.** For Russian checkers, it was **in 1895.**

3.3. Modern Board Games

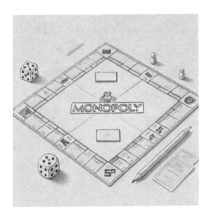

250. Have you ever played **Monopoly**? It is a super fun game, which was invented **in 1935** by a guy named **Charles Darrow**, but he was not the first person to come up with the idea. The idea for the game is based on an earlier version developed **in 1903** by **Elizabeth Magie**. The game was originally intended to show the harm of monopolies but later became a popular form of entertainment.

251. Today, Monopoly is published in more than **100 countries** and has been translated into **37 languages**.

252. Risk is a strategy board game created **in 1957** by French film director **Albert Lamorisse**. In the game, players control armies and try to conquer the world by moving troops across a map divided into territories. Risk became one of the first board games with global strategy and diplomacy, which made it popular around the world.

That is why it became so popular all over the world. It is still a classic game today, and they even have some versions based on movies and books like "Star Wars" and "The Lord of the Rings."

253. Imagine a game where you can be anyone you want and go on any adventure you can dream up! That is the magic of **Dungeons & Dragons**, the first tabletop role-playing game, which appeared **in 1974**. This game lets players create their characters and go on incredible journeys in a make-believe world. It was the start of a new type of game where players could be creative and use their brains to solve problems and overcome challenges.

254. In **the 1990s**, "Eurogames," also known as **German-style board games**, began to gain popularity in Europe, especially in Germany. These games have simple rules, strategy, and a minimal element of chance. Examples include **"Catan"** (1995) and **"Carcassonne"** (2000).

255. Catan is a board game created by German designer **Klaus Teuber in 1995**. The game quickly became one of the most popular in the world due to its combination of strategy, trade, and chance. By 2020, more than **32 million copies** of the game had been sold, and it had been translated into **40 languages**.

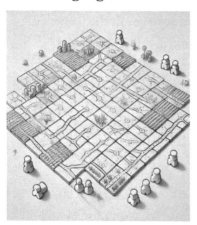

256. Carcassonne is a board game created by German designer **Klaus-Jürgen Wrede in 2000**. The game is named after the French city of Carcassonne and is about building medieval lands, roads, and cities.

257. Carcassonne is a board game that is all about building stuff. It got popular quickly because the rules are simple, but there are tons of different strategies you can use. By 2021, it had sold over **12 million copies**, which makes it one of the most well-known building games out there.

258. In the early 2000s, a new type of board game became popular: **cooperative games**! In these games, everyone plays on the same team and tries to win together. It is like everyone is on the same side. One example is "**Pandemic**," which was released in 2008.

259. Some games have a cool **theme and story**, like "**Arkham Horror**" and "**Space Truckers.**" These games are popular with people who like games that are a bit more challenging.

260. Scrabble is a popular board game where you make words out of letter tiles. It was invented in **1948** by an American guy named Alfred Mosher Butts. You get random letters and try to make the best words you can on a special board. Each letter is worth points, and the person with the most points wins.

Scrabble is a hit around the world, and people play it in **over 30 languages.** It is so popular that it is in **the Toy Hall of Fame!** There are even big Scrabble tournaments where people from all over the world compete. If you like word games, you should try Scrabble.

261. Scrabble has official versions in over **30 languages.** It is also used in schools to help kids learn new words. When you play Scrabble, you have to think about what words you can make, which helps you learn new words without even realizing it.

262. Scrabble is played all around the world. There is a thing called the **World Scrabble Federation,** a giant club for Scrabble players from all over the world. You can find Scrabble clubs for everyone, whether you are just a starter or a super pro. And if you do not want to leave your house, you can even play Scrabble online.

263. Clue (called **Cluedo** in some places) is a board game where you try to solve a mystery. It was invented **in 1944** by a British guy named **Anthony Pratt**. The game is a detective puzzle where players try to figure out who committed the murder, where, and with what weapon. The game is set in a big mansion.

Players move their chips around the board, collecting clues to eliminate possible options. Each player takes turns making a guess, and the other players show him cards if they have information that confirms or refutes this guess. Cluedo was one of the first detective games and quickly gained popularity. Since then, it has undergone many updates and has been released in various versions.

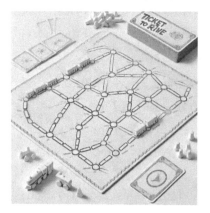

264. Have you ever played **Ticket to Ride**? It is a fun board game where you are to build your train routes! The game was invented **in 2004** by this guy from America, **Alan R. Moon**. You collect cards of different colors to build railroads between cities on a map. The player who builds the longest routes wins the game.

Ticket to Ride is super popular and has different versions for different parts of the world, like North America and Europe. It is easy to learn but also has lots of strategies.

3.4. Computer Games

265. Computer games are much older than you might think! They started way back **in the 1950s.** In the early 50s, someone created OXO, similar tic-tac-toe, and checkers. These were some of the first games that used computers to play. And then there was "**Tennis for Two**" in 1958. It appeared on a screen called an oscilloscope, and it was a simple tennis game.

266. **Spacewar!** was one of **the first video games** ever! It was created in 1962 by some college students in the United States. It became popular at universities and helped inspire many games after it. It was the first game where players could compete against each other and even had some **basic graphics.** It was a big step towards making more complex video games. The game had exciting gameplay with real-time action, making it a significant milestone in video game history.

267. **Pong is a very famous arcade game.** It came out in **1972** and was made by **Atari.** The person who designed it was **Nolan Bushnell.** It was the first successful video game that resembled tennis. You control a "paddle" and try to hit a ball back and forth. Pong got super popular and helped start the whole arcade video game industry. It is one of the most important games ever because it helped make video games so popular.

268. **In 1980**, Namco introduced Pac-Man to the arcade gaming world. It became one of the most famous arcade games ever! Toru Iwatani designed Pac-Man. It was different from other arcade games because it was not violent. The main character, Pac-Man, has to eat dots in a maze while avoiding ghosts.

269. **Pac-Man quickly became a major success and turned into a symbol of the 1980s.** It inspired numerous sequels and contributed to the rise of cool cultural stuff, like cartoons, toys, and other things you can buy.

270. **In 1981, Nintendo created Donkey Kong,** an arcade game. You get to play as **Mario,** and your job is to rescue a girl from this giant monkey named Donkey Kong. This game was Nintendo's first big hit and helped start the popular Mario game series.

271. In the 1980s, **Nintendo** released its **Nintendo Entertainment System (NES),** changing everything about video game consoles. It also helped bring video games back after a crisis in 1983, launching many classic game series, including **Super Mario** and **The Legend of Zelda.**

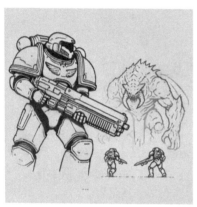

272. In the 1990s, 3D graphics started to become popular in video games. It led to more complex games like **Doom** (1993) and **Warcraft** (1994).

273. **The 1990s** were a time of great **changes** for fighting, racing, and strategy games. It was also when the first popular online games which allowed large groups of players to interact online appeared.

274. The 2000s were like a new era for video game consoles! We got some amazing new ones, like the **PlayStation 2** (made by **Sony** in 2000) and the **Xbox** (made by **Microsoft** in 2001). These consoles had better graphics and allowed lots of people to play together. They also started having online services for games, which changed the video game industry.

275. In the 2000s, **PCs** got even better for gaming. They had powerful processors and graphics cards that could handle complicated games. PCs became the main platform for strategy games, role-playing games, and online games where lots of people play together, like **World of Warcraft** and **Counter-Strike**.

276. In the 2010s, everyone started playing games on their phones and tablets. Mobile games like **Angry Birds** (2009) and **Clash of Clans** (2012) became super popular.

277. The 2010s also brought us modern games with awesome graphics and complex gameplay, like **The Witcher 3: Wild Hunt** (2015) and **Fortnite** (2017).

278. Minecraft is a game that came out **in 2011**. It lets you build and explore a world made of blocks. It is one of the best-selling games ever, with over **200 million copies** sold worldwide.

279. Grand Theft Auto V (2013) is an open-world game where you can explore a city, do missions, and race. It is one of the most successful games ever, making **over $6 billion**!

280. The Elder Scrolls V: Skyrim is a role-playing game where you can explore a huge fantasy world. It came out in 2011, and people love it because it has an interesting story and a super detailed world. It is become a classic for people who love role-playing games.

281. The Witcher 3: Wild Hunt (2015) is a role-playing game where you can explore an enormous open world based on books by Andrzej Sapkowski. The game is famous for its awesome story, graphics, and interesting characters. It also has won many awards.

282. What do you know of **Red Dead Redemption 2**? It is this super cool Western adventure game where you get to explore a large open world. It came out in 2018, and people love it because it looks so real and has an interesting story in the Wild West. It has won a bunch of awards and is a favorite among gamers.

4. Houses, Bridges, Cities, and Streets

4.1. The Oldest Buildings in the World

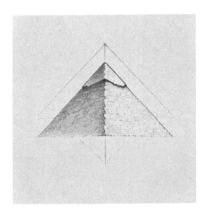

283. The Great Pyramid of Giza in Egypt is the biggest and one of the oldest structures in the world, built around **2580 BC** as a tomb for the pharaoh Khufu. It was one of the Seven Wonders of the Ancient World

284. Göbekli Tepe in Turkey is the oldest religious site in the world. It was built around **9600 BC**. This ancient sanctuary was probably used for religious ceremonies.

285. Have you ever heard of **Stonehenge**? It is in England, and it is this super cool thing made of giant stones. It was built a long time ago, between **3000 and 2000 BC**. People think it was used to watch the stars and as a place for religious ceremonies.

286. The Temple of Hatshepsut in Egypt was built around **1479 BC**, during the New Kingdom period, in honor of the pharaoh Hatshepsut. This wonderful structure has many terraces and columns.

287. The Ziggurat of Ur in Iraq is an ancient temple complex built around **2100 BC**. It was built to worship the god Nanna and was one of the greatest temples of the ancient world.

288. The Greek Theatre at Epidaurus was built in **the 4th century BC** and is considered one of the best-preserved theaters of Ancient Greece. It is famous for its amazing acoustics.

4.2. Old Bridges

289. Did you know that the Romans were super good at building **roads?** They built a massive network of roads, about 50,000 miles long, that covered all of Europe. Almost all modern roads and highways in Europe are built on Roman roads or follow their paths. Of course, so many roads led to the construction of many bridges. **Some of these ancient bridges built by the Romans still exist today.**

290. **The Romans built bridges out of stone or wood.** They used stone if the river had a strong current and wood if the river had a weak current. All the bridges had an arch shape as their main structure.

291. **The Alcántara Bridge in Spain** is an old Roman bridge built in the **1st century AD** across **the Tagus River** in **Alcántara,** a town in Spain. The bridge is made of stone and has six arches that are all the same size. It is about 600 feet long. The Romans used it for their armies and trading, making it vital for connecting different parts of their empire.

And guess what? You can still walk and drive across this bridge today! Its longevity is impressive, as it still stands today. It probably would have lasted even longer if people had not fought wars and damaged it. The bridge was partially destroyed several times during various wars but always restored. The name Alcántara means "bridge".

292. Have you ever heard of the **Ponte Milvio** in **Rome?** It is one of the most famous and oldest bridges there, built in **the 2nd century BC.** Many Roman emperors and conquerors entered Rome across this bridge. It was used by cars until 1956, but now it is just for people to walk. It is a super important piece of history, so many people visit it in Rome.

293. The Cendere Bridge in Turkey is an old Roman bridge. The Romans built it in **the 1st century AD** during the time of **Emperor Septimius Severus**. The bridge goes over the Cendere River. It is an excellent example of how good the Romans were as builders. It consists of these massive stone arches that are still strong today. The Cendere Bridge is one of the best-preserved Roman buildings in Turkey, and it is a significant place for people to learn about history.

294. The Ponte Pietra in Verona, Italy, is an old Roman bridge built in the 1st century BC spanning the Adige River. The bridge is 158 feet (48 meters) long and has five arches. It was partly destroyed during World War II but was rebuilt later. It is a significant historical landmark in the city.

295. The Ponte Vecchio is like a bridge and a shopping mall all in one! Located in **Florence, Italy.** It is one of the most famous and oldest bridges in Europe, built **in 1345**. The bridge crosses **the Arno River** and is **98 feet** long. What makes it unique is that it has houses built right on it.

These houses have been used as shops for a long time. Ponte Vecchio used to be a location where jewelers and other merchants had their shops, and it is still one of the most famous symbols of Florence.

296. The Arkadiko Bridge, also known as **the Kazarma Bridge**, is an ancient bridge near **Nafplion**, Greece. It was built in **3000 BC** and is one of the oldest stone bridges in the world that is still standing. The bridge was **part of an ancient road** that connected **Corinth** and other important cities in the Peloponnese. Engineers built the Arkadiko Bridge with an arch design, which made it strong and long-lasting. It is often called **the first known stone arch bridge**, which was important for future bridge construction. Today, the Arkadiko Bridge is a bright example of ancient Greek engineering and remains a popular tourist attraction.

297. The Caravan Bridge in Izmir is **about 3,000 years old**! It was first built **in 850 BC**, which makes it one of the oldest bridges still standing in the world. The bridge was a part of an old trading route, so it was important for connecting different places, like Mesopotamia, Egypt, and the Mediterranean. This bridge is a unique example of early bridge building and is an important historical site.

298. The Latin Bridge in Sarajevo, Bosnia and Herzegovina, is not as old as some other bridges we have talked about, but it is famous for a **historically significant** event. Built **in 1557,** the Latin Bridge goes over the Miljacka River. It is **49 feet long** and is considered a well-known landmark in the city. The Latin Bridge is known because it is where **Archduke Franz Ferdinand of Austria was killed in 1914,** which was one of the reasons **World War I** started. The bridge is still used today as a pedestrian bridge and is an important symbol of the city. There are 35 bridges across the river in Sarajevo.

299. The Anji Bridge was constructed in **605 AD in northern China** during **the Sui Dynasty.** It is **one of the oldest stone bridges in China** and is considered a great example of ancient Chinese engineering. It was built with **an arch design,** which made it very strong. This bridge has survived many floods and earthquakes without any damage.

4.3. Long Bridges

300. The Danyang–Kunshan Grand Bridge in China is one of the longest bridges in the world. It is 102.4 miles long and is part of the **Beijing–Shanghai** High-Speed Railway. The bridge was finished in 2010 and connects the cities of **Shanghai** and **Nanjing**.

It goes over swamps, lakes, and rivers, which makes it a major engineering achievement. This bridge allows trains to travel at high speeds, making the trip between these cities much faster.

301. The Changhua–Kaohsiung Viaduct in Taiwan is one of the longest bridges on the island. It was constructed to link **Changhua** and **Kaohsiung** with a high-speed rail line. The viaduct is 97.8 miles long and is a key part of **Taiwan's high-speed rail system**, making travel time between the two major cities much shorter.

302. The Tianjin Grand Bridge is like a super-long roller coaster for trains! Located in **China**, it is one of the longest and highest bridges in the world. It is 70.2 miles long. It is part of a super-fast train line that connects **Beijing** and **Shanghai**. The bridge was completed in **2011**. It goes over all sorts of different cities and areas, including **Tianjin** and other key places in China. It allows trains to travel at high speeds, improving transportation and reducing travel time between two of the largest cities in China, Beijing and Shanghai.

303. The Hong Kong–Zhuhai–Macau Bridge is like a highway spanning the ocean! It is **the longest sea bridge** in the world, connecting three cities: **Hong Kong, Zhuhai** (China), and **Macau**. It is 34 miles long. The bridge was officially opened in **2018**, and it is a significant part of a project to make it easier to travel around the **Greater Bay Area**.

The bridge is more than just a bridge: it consists of **different bridges, tunnels**, and even some **islands** made just for it. It makes traveling between Hong Kong, Macau, and Zhuhai much faster. It used to take hours on a boat, but now it only takes about **30 minutes** to cross the bridge!

304. Have you ever heard of **the Lake Pontchartrain Causeway**? It is a super long bridge in **Louisiana, USA**, and the longest bridge in North America. It is like a giant floating road stretching over **Lake Pontchartrain** and links **Metairie** and **New Orleans**. The bridge was opened in **1956**, and it is still an important way for people to travel between those two cities. It consists of two separate bridges, like having two lanes on a highway, and it is the longest bridge in the world that goes completely over water.

305. The Manchac Swamp Bridge is a super-long bridge in **Louisiana, USA,** and it is one of the longest bridges that goes over a swamp in the world. It is 22.8 miles long. The bridge was constructed in **1979**. It goes through one of the biggest swamps in the US, so it is like driving through a jungle full of water and trees. The way it is built makes it easy to travel across the swamp and get to major places in Louisiana fast.

4.4. Long Pedestrian Bridges

306. The Zhangjiajie Glass Bridge in China is a unique hanging bridge that is **the longest and highest glass bridge in the world**. It is like walking on a cloud made of glass! It opened in **2016** and is located 984 feet above a canyon in **Zhangjiajie National Forest Park**. The bridge is 1,410 feet long and 19.7 feet wide. It is like being in a movie where you can see everything below you, but this is real! You can walk on the clear glass and see the mountains and forests around you. It is a spectacular view but might be a little scary if you are afraid of heights.

307. The Charles Kuonen Suspension Bridge is like walking on a tightrope, but it is safe, and the views are incredible! Located in **Switzerland**, it is **one of the longest bridges in the world you can walk across**. It opened in **2017** in Valais, near a cool town called **Zermatt**. The bridge is

1,624 feet long and stands about 279 feet above the valley floor. It connects two popular hiking trails, and **the views of the mountains and the Alps** are absolutely breathtaking. This suspension bridge was built to improve mountain trails and provide hikers with more options for exploring.

308. Sky Bridge 721 in the Czech Republic is **a pedestrian bridge** located in Bohemian Switzerland, the national park in **the Czech Republic.** It opened in 2021 and is **the longest suspension bridge for walkers** in the Czech Republic. The bridge is 2,365 feet (721 meters) long and is located 312 feet above the valley. The bridge connects two rocky cliffs and offers tourists spectacular views of the natural beauty of the region, including deep canyons, forests, and mountains. This place has become popular with outdoor enthusiasts and those looking for a unique experience of walking across this sky bridge.

309. Gandaki Golden Bridge in Nepal is a pedestrian suspension bridge built across **the Gandaki River** in the **Himalayas.** The bridge is about **1,870 feet long** and has a beautiful **golden color**. It has become a popular tourist attraction because of its beautiful design and amazing views of the mountains and valleys. The bridge is open to visitors, offering a safe way for people to cross the river in this mountainous area. Everyone loves how unique it looks, like something out of a movie!

4.5. Old Buildings Where People Still Live or Work

310. Nishiyama Onsen Keiunkan in Japan is **the oldest hotel in the world**, operating since its founding by the **Oyama** family in **705 AD**. It is situated in a beautiful area near **Fuji**. The hotel is known for its hot springs (onsens) and traditional Japanese architecture. Nishiyama Onsen Keiunkan has received recognition by **the Guinness World Records** for the longest-running period of operation under the same family.

311. The Bridge Tea Rooms was established in **1502** and is **the oldest tea room in the UK** that is still operating. It has a long history and is an important part of Britain's cultural heritage, providing a unique atmosphere and traditional tea service.

312. Banca Monte dei Paschi di Siena is the oldest bank in the world, and it has been around since **1472**! It was established to provide small loans to help the locals in difficult times. Since its founding, the bank has gone through many historical events and changes. However, it still plays a role in the financial system of Italy.

313. Have you ever heard of the **village of Kirkjubøur** in the **Faroe Islands?** It is on a small island called **Streymoy,** and it is famous for having this **super old wooden house** that people used to live in.

It was built about 1,000 years ago, which is seriously ancient! It is **one of the oldest wooden houses still around in all of Europe.**

314. The Doesburgermolen is like a time machine that takes you back to the 1600s! It is a windmill in a place called **Ede in the Netherlands,** and it is one of the oldest windmills still around. It was constructed around **1630,** which is seriously old. People used to grind grain and other farming needs. The Doesburgermolen has survived and continues to operate, making it an important cultural landmark. The mill also serves as a symbol of historical rural life and the engineering skills of the Netherlands, where windmills played a key role in the lives of local people.

4.6. The tallest buildings

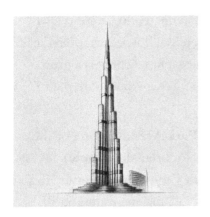

315. The Burj Khalifa is like a giant LEGO tower that reaches to the sky! It is in Dubai, and it is the tallest building in the world. It is 2,717 feet tall. It was finished in 2010 and has 163 floors. There are places where you can go to check out the view, and there are also fancy apartments and offices inside.

The Burj Khalifa is a symbol of how impressive modern design and engineering can be. Although, who knows, by the time you are reading this, they might have built something even taller.

316. Merdeka 118 is a skyscraper in **Kuala Lumpur, Malaysia**. It is super tall: 2,227 feet high! It is the second tallest building in the world, which is amazing! It was constructed in 2021 and is the tallest building in Malaysia. Inside, Merdeka 118 has offices where people work, apartments where people live, and hotel rooms for visitors. It is like a mini-city inside! Merdeka 118 is a sign of how Kuala Lumpur is growing and changing.

317. Shanghai Tower is a super tall building in **Shanghai, China**. It is super tall: 2,073 feet high. It is one of the tallest buildings in the world. That is super cool! The construction was completed in 2015 and is a symbol of modern China. The tower contains 128 floors with offices,

hotel rooms, and even places where you can go to see an amazing view of the city. It is like a whole city in one building! It also has a twisty shape.

318. The Clock Towers is a group of super-tall buildings in Mecca, Saudi Arabia. One of the buildings is super tall, **1,971 feet**, called **the Abraj Al-Bait Tower**. It is one of the tallest buildings in the world, and it is also the heaviest building in the world. Inside, there is a hotel, a shopping mall, and a place where you can learn about Islamic culture. There is a giant clock at the top of the tallest building. You can see it from more than **17 miles away!**

319. 432 Park Avenue is one of the tallest residential skyscrapers in New York City, United States. It is 1,396 feet tall, making it the fourth tallest building in New York City and the second tallest residential building in the world. The tower is a part of the prestigious Manhattan neighborhood. 432 Park Avenue includes luxury residential apartments with windows that provide panoramic views of the city.

4.7. Unusual buildings

320. The Thin House is an unusual building in London, England, located in a neighborhood called **Notting Hill**. What makes it so unique? It is incredibly narrow! At its narrowest point, it is only about **7.5 feet** wide. That makes it one of the skinniest houses in the world! The Thin House was built long ago, in the late 1800s. It is shaped that way because it was built in an extremely small space between other buildings. Even though it is so narrow, it is a real house with everything a family needs.

321. The Big Basket is an office building in **Lancaster, Ohio**. It is the headquarters of the Longaberger Company, which makes baskets. The building looks like a giant picnic basket, about seven floors tall. It is one of the most famous and unusual buildings in the United States.

322. The Upside-Down building in **Pigeon Forge, Tennessee, USA,** is a weird and wacky tourist attraction. It is a real house, built **upside down**, with the roof on the ground and the foundation in the air.

Everything in the house, including furniture, decor, and rooms, is upside down, making visitors feel like they are in a world where the laws of physics seem impossible. The house is a popular destination for tourists looking for unusual photo spots.

323. Have you ever seen a building that looks like it belongs in a painting? The **Torre Galatea** in **Figueres, Spain,** is just like that! It is a surreal building, making it look like something out of a dream. It is part of the **Dalí Theatre and Museum**, which is all about the art of Salvador Dalí. Dalí was a remarkable painter who liked to paint strange and unusual things. He designed the Torre Galatea himself, and it was his home and studio for many years. The tower is covered in giant **yellow eggs**, one of Dalí's favorite symbols. The museum was founded in 1974 and is now one of the most visited museums in Spain, housing a collection of paintings, sculptures, and other works of art created by Dalí.

324. **The Kansas City Public Library** in **Missouri** is an impressive building! It looks like a giant wall of books! **The front of the library** is covered in **huge pictures of book covers**, like large versions of **popular books**. The library is a symbol of knowledge and culture, and it is a popular destination for tourists and locals alike.

4.8. Ancient Cities That are Still Inhabited

325. Damascus, Syria, is a really, really old city. Actually, it is **one of the oldest cities in the whole world** where people still live! It is even the oldest capital city in the world, with a history of over 11,000 years! Damascus was an important place for trade and culture a long, long time ago, and it still is today.

It is where many old trading routes crossed, so it was a key place for many different groups of people, like the Arameans, Romans, Byzantines, and Muslims. The old part of Damascus is so special that it is on the UNESCO World Heritage List.

326. Jericho, in **Palestine**, is one of the oldest cities ever! It is super old, like maybe 10,000 or 11,000 years old. You can even read about it in the Bible. It is near the Dead Sea, in a place known as an oasis, where there is water and plants in the middle of the desert. Jericho was a great place for farming because of the water and good soil. It is also the lowest city in the world, about 820 feet below sea level!

327. Aleppo, Syria, is **another super old city**, over 8,000 years old! It was a major center for trade and culture. The land around Aleppo was great for growing things like wheat, dates, and olives. But, because it was such a valuable city, it has been attacked many times throughout history. Romans, Turks, Mongols, and others all took control of Aleppo at some point. As a result, Aleppo's architecture is a fascinating blend of different styles.

328. Byblos (or **Jbeil**) is an old city in **Lebanon**. It is one of the oldest cities in the world that is still inhabited. People lived there as far back as 8000 BC, but it became a major city around **5000 BC**. Byblos was a major trading and cultural center, especially for the Phoenicians. They were famous sailors and traders who spread the alphabet from Byblos to many other places. Today, Byblos is **a UNESCO World Heritage Site.** It means that the city is recognized by UNESCO as a place of great historical importance.

329. Athens is **the capital of Greece** and one of the oldest cities in the world, with **over 3,000 years** of history. Athens was the center of **ancient Greek civilization** and home to famous philosophers like **Socrates, Plato,** and **Aristotle**. The Acropolis of Athens is an ancient archaeological complex, which includes monuments such as the **Parthenon, Erechtheion,** and **the Temple of Athena Nike.** The Acropolis is a symbol of ancient Greek culture, making it one of the most visited attractions in the world. Athens is also famous for being the first place where people got to vote and make decisions about their city - that is called **democracy.**

330. Yerevan, the capital of **Armenia,** is **one of the oldest cities** in the world, with about 3,000 years of history. It was founded in **782 BC** by **King Argishti I,** and it has become an important cultural and political center of the region. One of the most famous landmarks of the city is the **Cascade,** a tiered staircase connecting the central districts of the city with the upper ones. It provides a magnificent view of Yerevan and Mount **Ararat.**

331. Beijing is a very old city with over **3,000** years of history. It was founded in **the 11th century BC.** Over the years, Beijing has been the capital of many different Chinese dynasties. It has played a key role in the development of Chinese culture, politics, and economy. Today, it remains the most important cultural and political center of China.

4.9. Huge Cities

332. Tokyo is a huge city in **Japan**, and it is actually the biggest city in the whole world! **Over 37 million people** live there. Tokyo is a mix of the old and the new. You can find super modern technology alongside traditional Japanese culture. It is also the most important city in Japan for business and culture.

333. Have you ever heard of **Delhi, India?** It is one of the biggest cities in the world and has **over 31 million people** living there. Delhi is full of amazing things to see and do. It is the heart of India's politics, culture, and history. You can explore ancient monuments and find a variety of modern shopping centers.

334. Did you know that Delhi has a special part called **New Delhi**? It is the capital of India! The British decided it would be **the capital in 1911** when they had just finished planning the city. You can find important government buildings, embassies, and other significant places there.

335. Shanghai, China, is one of the most populated cities in the world! Around **27 million** people live there. Shanghai is a major financial and trade center for China. It is famous for its tall buildings and the biggest port in the world.

4.10. Capitals of the World

336. Washington, D.C., District of Columbia, is the capital of the United States. It is unique because it does not belong to any state. The idea was to ensure that no single state had too much influence over the capital. Washington D.C. was founded in 1790 and named after the first president of the United States, George Washington.

337. The capital of China, Beijing, has changed its name 19 times! Primarily depending on the political situation. The last changes were in the 20th century. In **1912**, after the founding of the Republic of China, it was renamed **Beijing**, which in Chinese means "Northern Capital." In **1958**, the Chinese government decided to change the name to **Beiping** in the context of language simplification. However, in 1969, the name was restored to Beijing.

338. Did you know that South Africa has not one, not two, but **three capitals**? It is kind of unusual, but each city plays a different role:
- **Pretoria**: Think of Pretoria as **the seat of government.** It is where the President and other important government officials work.
- **Cape Town**: This is where **the laws** are created and passed. Parliament meets in Cape Town to discuss and pass new laws for South Africa.
- **Bloemfontein**: This is where **the highest court** in the country is located. The judges in Bloemfontein make important decisions about the laws.

339. Tanzania actually has **two capitals: Dar es Salaam** and **Dodoma.** Dar es Salaam is the administrative capital, where the government offices are, while Dodoma is the legislative capital, where the parliament meets. This division was established in 1974 when the government decided to move the parliament to Dodoma to stimulate the development of the country's interior.

340. Rome, Italy, is a really special city because **it has another country inside it!** That country is **Vatican City,** and it is the only country in the world that is **surrounded by another city.** Vatican City is the center of the Roman Catholic Church, and it is super tiny, only 0.2 square kilometers! That makes it the smallest country in the world.

341. If you are an animal enthusiast, you will not want to miss the **Berlin Zoo!** Situated in Germany's capital, this zoo boasts the world's largest collection of animals, with over **20,000 residents** from **1,300 different species.** Established in **1844,** it is a popular attraction for tourists seeking a unique wildlife experience.

342. **Mexico City,** the capital of Mexico, is home to **one-fifth of the country's entire population.** With **over 9 million people,** it is not only the largest city in Mexico but also one of the most crowded big cities in the world.

343. **Copenhagen,** the capital of Denmark, is a city where **bicycles rule the streets.** More than **40%** of the people living there use bikes to get around every day. It makes Copenhagen one of the most **bike-crazy** cities you will ever find. They have awesome bike paths and are working hard to make the city a better place by encouraging people to bike instead of drive.

344. Imagine a city built on **14 islands** linked together by more than **50 bridges**! That is Stockholm, the capital of Sweden. You will find it on the **Skagerrak Strait,** and the way it is built on islands makes Stockholm a truly unique place where nature and buildings come together in a stunning way.

345. **Helsinki,** the capital of Finland, is super far north! In fact, it is **the most northern capital city on the continent.** It is located **at 60° north,** which makes it the most northern capital of any country on the continent.

346. **Reykjavik,** the capital of **Iceland,** is located even further north than Helsinki. It sits at **64° north,** making it the northernmost capital city in the world. And it is on an island because Iceland is an island.

347. **In Australia,** two big cities, **Sydney** and **Melbourne,** wanted to be the capital. But they could not agree, so they decided to build **a brand new city** that would be a neutral place for everyone. That is how **Canberra** was chosen in **1908** to become the capital. Canberra was planned to be in a good location and designed to meet the needs of the whole country without favoring either of the big cities.

4.11. Unusual Cities

348. Venice, Italy, is built on **118 small islands in a lagoon.** Venice has no cars, so the locals get around by rowing boats and gondolas. It makes Venice a unique and romantic place for tourists.

349. Port Lincoln, in **South Australia,** is a **diver's dream**! It is one of the top places to go diving in the area. The water is **crystal clear,** perfect for seeing all kinds of amazing sea creatures. You can even dive with **sharks**! And there are tons of **reefs and underwater parks** to explore.

350. When **divers** are underwater, they cannot talk, so they use hand signals. One of the most important signals is the **"OK"** sign. It is when you make a circle with your thumb and pointer finger. This tells other divers that everything is good and they are ready to continue the dive.

351. China is a country with many big cities! It has more cities with over a million people than any other country. There are **over 100** of these **"million-person cities"** in China. China's economy has grown quickly, and more people have moved to cities. Some of the biggest cities are **Shanghai, Beijing, Guangzhou,** and **Shenzhen.**

352. If you are looking for a truly unique place to visit, check out **Chefchaouen** (or **Chauen**). It is a town in **Morocco** that is famous for its **blue streets and buildings.** Located in the **northwestern part of the country,** in the mountains, it attracts tourists with its unique atmosphere. In Chefchaouen, all the houses and streets are painted in shades of blue, creating a beautiful and relaxing vibe.

One theory says that the blue color helps protect against heat and insects. While some people think it symbolizes the sky and its connection to spirituality. Today, Chefchaouen is a popular tourist destination, attracting people who want to enjoy the beautiful views and unique atmosphere of this historic town.

353. In the United States, there are a few cities named after European capitals. For example, there is a **London** in **Ohio** and a **London** in **Texas**. There are also two towns called **Moscow**, one in **Iowa** and one in **North Carolina**. And if you are looking for **Paris**, there is one in **Texas**! It is famous for having a **mini Eiffel Tower**.

354. Have you ever heard of a city that is underground? **Derinkuyu** in **Turkey** is just like that! It is an ancient city **carved into the rock** and used as a secret hiding place. Derinkuyu has eight **different levels** and is so big that it could hold up to **20,000** people! It was built a long, long time ago, **around the 7th century BC**, and it helped people stay safe from attacks. It even had ways to get fresh air, water wells, and many different rooms. People visit this amazing underground city to see how it was built.

355. Coober Pedy is a unique town in **Australia,** located in the **desert, north of South Australia**. It is famous because most of its inhabitants live in underground houses. This is due to the hot climate, where temperatures in summer can exceed **104°F**. Underground houses help maintain a comfortable temperature and protect against the heat. Coober Pedy is also known for its opals. It is one of the best places in the world to find these beautiful gemstones. That is why people came to live there initially, and they started building their homes underground to escape the heat. Today, you can find all sorts of things underground in Coober Pedy, including churches, shops, and even hotels! It is a cool place to explore.

356. There are many ancient cities around the world where people still live today. But many cities have been **abandoned**. These cities were once full of people and activity. However, for different reasons (like wars, natural disasters, or changes in the economy) everyone left. One of these abandoned cities is **Varosha** in Cyprus. It used to be a popular vacation spot, but after the Turkish invasion in **1974**, it was completely evacuated. Now, it is surrounded by fences and guarded by soldiers, and all the buildings, shops, and houses are empty. It is like a ghost town.
Even though it was abandoned, Varosha was still controlled by **the Turkish army**. Recently people have started talking about fixing it and opening it to visitors.

357. **Pripyat, Ukraine**, is another example of a city that is no longer inhabited. It was built **in 1970** specifically for the workers of the nearby Chernobyl Nuclear Power Plant. In 1986, the infamous Chernobyl disaster took place, forcing everyone to evacuate the city in just a few hours. Pripyat became a ghost town and remains so today, located within the **restricted Chernobyl Exclusion Zone**. Despite being abandoned, Pripyat draws in tourists and researchers, curious to see the abandoned buildings and the remnants of what was once a bustling city. **The Ferris wheel, the clock tower**, and **the empty apartments** stand as haunting reminders of the tragedy that occurred there.

358. **There is even a computer game dedicated to the Chernobyl disaster - S.T.A.L.K.E.R.** The game series in **the shooter genre** with elements of **role-playing** and **survival** takes place in an alternate reality where a second explosion occurred at the **Chernobyl nuclear power plant**. This explosion resulted in anomalies, mutated creatures, and other supernatural phenomena. The player controls a **stalker**, a person who explores these dangerous zones, fights mutants, and looks for valuable artifacts.

359. Terlingua is a small town in **Texas, USA**. It was a lively place in the early 20th century, thanks to the mining of a mineral containing mercury. But the mercury mines closed in the 1940s, and the town was abandoned. Today, Terlingua is a popular tourist destination, known for its **historic abandoned buildings and old mines**.

360. Pompeii is an ancient Roman city located in **Italy**, near **Naples**, which was destroyed in **79 AD** by the eruption of **Mount Vesuvius**. The city was covered with a thick layer of ash and lava, which allowed many buildings, streets, frescoes, and household items to be preserved in perfect condition for more than 1,900 years. Archaeological excavations of Pompeii began in **the 18th century.** Since then the city has become one of the most significant archaeological sites in the world, attracting millions of tourists. The city provides a unique insight into the life of the Romans of that time, with preserved houses, markets, and temples, as well as detailed frescoes and mosaics. Today, **Pompeii** is a UNESCO World Heritage Site, and excavations continue, revealing new secrets and details about the life of the ancient city and its tragic death.

4.12. Amazing Streets

361. Spreuerhofstraße in **Reutlingen, Germany,** is one of the narrowest streets in the world. At its narrowest point, it is only **12.2 inches wide,** and at its widest, it is about **19.7 inches wide.** The street was built in **1727** after a devastating fire in the city and is still a full-fledged street, marked on the city map.

362. Yonge Street in **Toronto, Canada,** is the longest street in the world. It stretches for **1,178 miles** and connects the city of Toronto with the northern areas of Ontario, passing through several provinces. Yonge Street was originally constructed as a road connecting Toronto with remote settlements and played a significant role in Canada's transportation system.

363. Want to see the widest street in the world? You will have to go to Brasilia, Brazil! The Monumental Axis is so wide, it is almost like a runway for airplanes. It was designed by a famous architect named Lucio Costa to make Brasilia a special, important city.

364. The Via Dolorosa is like a walk through history. It is also meaningful for Christians. It is in **Jerusalem,** and it is the street where, according to what Christians believe, Jesus carried his cross on the way to be crucified. The path is about 0.4 miles long, and it goes through the Old City of Jerusalem. There are 14 different places where Jesus stopped along the way, and each one reminds people of something important that happened to Jesus on his last journey. The Via Dolorosa is a significant place for religious people, and thousands of them come here every year to walk this path, especially during **Holy Week.**

365. **Lombard Street in San Francisco, USA,** is the crookedest street in the world. This street, only **0.25 miles long**, is famous for its eight sharp turns, making it unique and popular with tourists.

Leave the review

As an independent author with a small marketing budget, reviews are my livelihood on this platform. If you enjoyed this book, I'd really appreciate it if you left your honest feedback on Amazon.

I love hearing from my readers and I personally read every single review.

Made in United States
Troutdale, OR
05/05/2025

31113869R00060